HOW TO BUILD

The Ocean Pointer

A Strip-Built 19'6" Outboard Skiff

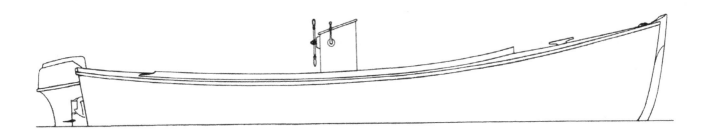

by David Stimson

A WoodenBoat Book

Note: The instructions in this book require the use of complete construction plans, David Stimson, Stimson Marine, RR1 River Road, Boothbay, Maine 04537

Book cover and text design by Tim Seymour Designs, LLC

All photographs by David Stimson

© 2002 by WoodenBoat Publications, Inc.
All rights reserved. Except for use in reviews, no part of this work may be reproduced or utilized in any form or by any means, electronic or mechanical, including photocopying, recording, or by any information storage and retrieval system, without written permission from the publisher.

Published by:
WoodenBoat Publications, Inc.
Naskeag Road, P.O. Box 78
Brooklin, Maine 04616 USA
1-800-273-7447
www.woodenboat.com

Printed in the USA   2

Library of Congress Cataloging-in-Publication Data
Stimson, David, 1954-
  How to build the Ocean Pointer :
a 19'6" outboard skiff / by David Stimson.
     p. cm.
  Includes bibliographical references.
  ISBN 0-937822-72-8
    1. Outboard motorboats—Design and construction.
    2. Skiffs—Design and construction.
    3. Boatbuilding. I. Title.

VM348 .S75 2002
623.8'2313—dc21

2002028871

DAVID STIMSON grew up on Cape Cod, Massachusetts, and learned boatbuilding while working in the local boatyards. During this time, he developed an eye for boat design from Merton Long, a retired catboat builder who became his friend and mentor. David's love of traditional boats was further inspired by the writings of John Gardner and Pete Culler in the 1970s, and by *WoodenBoat* magazine. He now lives in Boothbay, Maine, with his wife, Tamora and two teenage boys, Abraham and Nathaniel. He is a sailing charter captain during the summer, and designs and builds boats at Stimson Marine, Inc. in Boothbay.

Acknowledgments

I would like to thank Peter Spectre for his guidance during the early phases of this book, Jane Crosen for her editing and proofing, and the good folks at WoodenBoat Books for helping with the final production. All of you readers are indebted to Tom Hodgson for reading the manuscript and mercilessly cutting out the clichés. I happen to like clichés. Oh well, that's the way the cookie crumbles....

— David Stimson

Introduction

From West Pointer to Ocean Pointer 1
Ocean Pointer's design and construction 4

I Design and Performance

To vee or not to vee:
A question of flat bottom vs. deadrise 5
Ocean Pointer's hull lines,
and how they affect performance 6

II Getting Started

Setting up your shop 9
A Building Platform 9
Tools 9
Lighting 9
Pencils 10
Heat 10
Safe use of power tools 10
Safe handling of epoxy 11
Tips for successful gluing 11
Construction overview 13
Materials and supplies 14

III Making Molds and Patterns

Materials 15
Making the cockpit molds 15
Patternmaking 15

IV The Backbone: Keel, Stem, and Transom

Materials 17
Inner and outer keel 17
The inner stem 18
The outer stem 19
The forefoot 19
The transom 20

V Making the Bulkhead Frames and Setting Up

Materials 21
Bulkhead frames and motorwell sides 21
The cockpit sole 21
The ceiling 22
Setting up the molds 22
Marking the stations and
setting up the cockpit molds 22
Installing the motorwell sides and
bracing the molds 23
Installing the cockpit sole and transom 23
Installing the ceiling 24
Installing the bulkhead frames 25
Installing the inner keel 25
Installing the stem 26
Applying epoxy fillets 26
Installing the outer keel 26
Beveling the bulkhead frames 26
Beveling the forward end of the inner keel 27
Beveling the transom 27
Sealing the plywood 27
Installing the control cable and wiring conduits 27
Installing the Styrofoam flotation 28

VI Planking

Materials 29
Removing the temporary fastenings 29
Preparing the plank strips 29
Planking the hull 29
Applying the fillets 31
Cutting off the planking parallel to the sheer 31

VII Completing the Exterior

Materials 33
Fairing the hull 33
Installing the outer stem and forefoot 35
Flipping the boat 36

VIII Preparing for Decking

Materials	37
Planing the sheer	37
Fitting and fastening the inner rubrails	37
Dynel cockpit sheathing	39
The deck framing	39

IX Laying the Deck

Materials	43
Marking and cutting out the deck panels	43
Installing the deck panels	43
Sheathing the deck with Dynel	44

X Completing the Woodwork

Materials	45
Building the center console and seat box	46
Building the forward seat	46
Making the coamings	46
The outer rubrails	49
Striking the waterline	49
The spray rails	49

XI Controls, Deck Hardware, and Finishing

Materials	51
Mounting the hardware	51
The helm	52
The control lever	52
The control cables	52
The splashwell mounting kit	53
Scupper drains	53
Running lights	53
Ventilators	53
Bow chocks	53
Panel and battery switch	53
Ignition switch	53
Mooring and stern cleats	54
Fire extinguisher	54
Installing the console	54
Installing the seat box	54
The battery box	54
The wiring	54
The fuel tanks	54
Choosing a motor	54
Painting and varnishing	55
Finishing touches	55

Appendix I: Sources for Materials

Marine supplies, hardware, paint, epoxy	56
Marine plywood	56
White cedar strips, 1/8-inch mahogany veneer, oak, ash, and mahogany	56
Full-sized patterns for Ocean Pointer	56
Dynel fabric	56

Appendix II: Repairs and Maintenance

Repairing the hole	57
Repairing the damaged stem	57
Maintenance	57

Introduction

ON A FALL DAY IN 1988 I was busily planing on a plank when the crisp sound and pungent aroma of cedar shavings suddenly became drowned by the rumble and smell of a diesel engine. I laid down my plane and stepped out the door to see my friend Michael McConnell emerging from the cab of his lobster truck. He had a copy of *National Fisherman* under his arm, and a faraway gleam in his eye. I instantly recognized the signs of "acute boat affliction," and ushered him into the boatshop to see whether it was something that could be cured. A snow shovel made quick work of the messy workbench. This made room for the *Fisherman*, which he spread out, opening to a neat article about an old-timer named Alton Wallace who was known along the Maine coast for his West Pointer work skiffs. Mr. Wallace had apparently originated the Pointer hull about fifty years previously, and had built more than two hundred of them since then. Pointing to a photograph of one of Wallace's handsome 18-footers, Michael asked, "Can you build me one of these about 20 feet long?"

My eyes must have glazed over for a few moments as I pondered the possibility of actually building a new boat. As is the case with many builders, most of our bread-and-butter work had been in repair and restoration, and new commissions were few and far between. I reentered the Earth's atmosphere in time to hear Michael say that Wallace was selling his 18-footers for $3,500, and how much would I charge for a 20-foot version? After some rough figuring, I blurted out a figure that would ultimately bring in an hourly wage at the low end of poverty level, and the seed for Ocean Pointer was planted.

From West Pointer to Ocean Pointer

Before designing Michael's boat, I wanted to go talk to Alton Wallace, and see his boats "in the flesh." This was arranged with a phone call, and Michael and I set off for West Point, a village just down the Kennebec River from Bath. Forty-five minutes later we pulled into the driveway of the old West Point schoolhouse which Mr. Wallace had converted into a boatshop many years before. We weren't sure what to expect for a reception, and wondered how Alton would feel about giving information to "the competition." We needn't have worried; at the price Wallace was charging for his skiffs, there was no competition, and he knew it. Lack of customers was never a problem, so we were not considered to be a threat to his livelihood. Even so, Alton had nothing to gain from our visit except a wasted morning, and it was good of him to take time to show us around his shop, and tell us about his West Pointers. He generously allowed us to measure the beam and depth of a Pointer that he was just finishing, and showed us a half model and a number of nicely made duck decoys that he had carved. Not wanting to wear out our welcome, we thanked him for his help and generosity and headed home to Boothbay.

Armed with information and inspiration, I drew a rough profile on a block of wood, got out my gouges, mallet, and spokeshave, and began carving a half model for my own rendition of the Pointer. After the model had been shaped to my satisfaction, the lines for the design would be lifted from the model, and a scale drawing made in three different sectional views representing the three-dimensional shape of the model in two dimensions.

I should explain to newcomers to the boatbuilding tradition that carving a half model is an old-fashioned way of designing the hull shape for a boat. I prefer to design boats this way because it allows me to view the hull from different angles and see details that might not be apparent in a flat drawing. For example, a sheerline that appears fair in a profile drawing may appear "moose shouldered" or humped near the bow when the boat is built. This illusion arises because the curve of the sheer in the three-dimensional boat is a combination of two curves—the profile and the plan view. When we look at the boat from different angles, the apparent curve of the sheer may be quite different from the way it looks on paper.

After I had carved the model for the Pointer, I took the lines off by bending a thin lead bar around the model at evenly spaced locations called stations. The shape of the model at each station was transferred to the paper to create the body plan view, and then the other two views were drawn and faired.

While working on the lines drawing, I began thinking about how the new boat was to be constructed. Wallace's boats were certainly well built for working craft, but I could see a number of details in the construction that might contribute to an early demise. Don't get me wrong; Alton Wallace was a skilled builder, and although he is no longer with us, many of his boats will go on working well into the twenty-first century.

Alton Wallace, like all good builders, built for a specific market. Above all else, the price had to be low. He got away with construction that was less than yacht quality because of the way his boats are used. The construction changes that I have implemented in Ocean Pointer make her much more suitable for the weekend pleasure boater, but the price of the finished boat is considerably higher than what Wallace charged. There is no doubt in my mind that if money had been no object, Alton could also have made use of marine plywood, Dynel cloth, and epoxy resin to make the West Pointer a better pleasure boat. He likely would have sent the customer to another builder instead, as he preferred to work with pine and oak. Alton had found his niche in life many years before, and was content to do what he was doing without feeling the need to experiment with new ideas and materials. I often wonder if I haven't made a wrong turn myself, when I find that I'm into the epoxy up to my elbows.

To keep the cost down, Wallace put his West Pointers together "dry"; that is, without bedding compounds, adhesives, or sealants. A well-built pleasure boat of traditional construction will have all faying surfaces (surfaces where wood meets wood) painted and set in bedding compound to help keep water out of the joints. This is time consuming, and adds appreciably to the initial cost of the boat. All the joints on Ocean Pointer were either glued with epoxy, or painted and bedded.

Along with their backbone and framing, the West Pointers' narrow pine strip planking was also laid dry, with galvanized finish nails driven edgewise to fasten one plank to the next. The boats would need to "soak up" for several days after launching, after which time they might or might not stop leaking. (I later met a couple of West Pointer owners who had to bail their boats daily.) It is not a big problem for the fisherman to bail a bucketful or two every morning before setting out, but a week of leaking combined with a rainfall could swamp an idle skiff and drown the motor, to the dismay of the weekend boater.

Workboats like the West Pointer tend to live longer if they are used daily. Frequent use keeps the topsides wet so that all the joints stay tight. If these same boats are left on a mooring five or six days a week, the sun will dry out the topsides and decks, opening seams and inviting rainwater to do its destructive work.

The West Pointer's galvanized nails were prone to rusting, and a tired old boat would be difficult to refasten. West Pointer hulls were definitely on the limber side. The lack of bulkheads and a small deck area contributed to this, as did the drylaid planking. When a hull is built without glue or caulking in the seams, the planks are able to slip with respect to one another, allowing the hull to change shape more readily than one whose planks are rigidly tied together. I chose Northern white cedar instead of pine for the planking for Ocean Pointer. It shrinks and swells less, and its compressibility is helpful when it does change dimension with fluctuations in moisture. The planking was edge-glued with epoxy, and edge-nailed with bronze ring nails.

Wallace's boats had frames of steam-bent oak. Although steam-bending is probably one of the best methods for framing a traditional hull, bent frames do have a few shortcomings. They are prone to breaking or cracking at the hardest turn of the bilge, and dirt and moisture tend to get trapped between the frames and the hull, eventually causing deterioration of the wood. It is also quite a project if one wishes to install a self-bailing cockpit in a hull that is traditionally framed. In Ocean Pointer, I decided to use plywood bulkhead frames instead of steam-bent oak frames. The framing for the cockpit sole, ceiling, and forward seat was all incorporated into the shape of the bulkhead frames, and even the deck crown was lofted in. The plywood frames became "webs" that rigidly connected the hull, deck, and cockpit structure to create a "truss" effect. The finished boat is so stiff, it rings like a bell when it is struck with a mallet.

The deck and cockpit of Ocean Pointer could best be described as "clean." There is hardly any place where moisture or dirt can collect. Dynel (an acrylic fabric sheathing similar to fiberglass) set in epoxy ensures that water will drain overboard, and not into the bilge. The self-bailing cockpit is surrounded by Styrofoam flotation, and the boat won't sink, even if the hull is badly holed. I had been telling people this for years without having proof until an Ocean Pointer owner obligingly hit a steel navigational buoy head-on at 15 knots (name of owner withheld to protect the embarrassed). After the initial impact, the boat rode up into the air and came down on top of the buoy, punching a 4-by-8-inch hole in the bottom of the boat. Fortunately, no one was hurt, and the flotation did its work. Amazingly, the cockpit never flooded. After the mishap the boat was motored home and tied to the dock, where she floated for several days just below her normal waterline before being hauled for the winter. I had always read that strip-planked boats were difficult to repair. In fact, I found the opposite to be true. The following spring, it took only six hours to repair the hole and the face of the stem, which was damaged superficially. Details of the repair can be found in Appendix II.

Alton Wallace died not long after the first Ocean Pointer was built, so I never got a chance to show it to him. It's hard to say whether he would have approved of the changes I made. Perhaps he would have thought it silly to put so much extra time and money into glorifying a workboat. Working craft have almost always been built cheaply, to be used hard for a number of years, and when too tired to work they are hauled up the beach to settle comfortably back into the earth that engendered them. There is something appealing about the naturalness of this cycle and of the boats themselves, a quality that is lost when modern life-extending petrochemicals are incorporated. That is why I haven't referred to my construction changes as improvements, preferring instead to call them modifications.

An Ocean Pointer should last a lot longer than a West Pointer, with less annual maintenance. But the cost of using modern materials and techniques is reflected in a higher initial price, and in the loss of a certain "soul" or character that graces the original boats. Alton Wallace's boats were an extension of his own soul and character. I really admired him, not only for developing the West Pointer, but for the way he lived, worked, and died happily in the tradition into which he was born. Thank you, Alton, for providing me with the inspiration for Ocean Pointer's model, and more importantly, with a model for living and working according to one's beliefs.

Ocean Pointer's design and construction

There is nothing new about the elements of Ocean Pointer's design or construction. The general hull form has been around for at least fifty years. Plywood bulkhead frames, strip planking, sheathing fabrics, and epoxy have been in use for decades. The combination of these elements is what makes Ocean Pointer unique. Someone may prove me wrong, but as of this writing, I think that this is the only design that incorporates epoxy-glued strip planking on bulkhead frames in a Pointer-style hull.

Longevity, low maintenance, light weight, and stiffness are obvious advantages. Another advantage is ease of construction for amateur builders. The use of plywood for the framing means that almost every important piece can be (and is) laid out on full-sized pattern sheets. There is no need to struggle through lofting—a process whereby the hull lines are laid down on a flat, level floor, full size, in order to determine the shape of the molds. Planking can be time consuming by whatever method chosen, but strip-planking does not require the knowledge or skill that is needed for conventional plank-on-frame methods. The use of short, narrow stock makes clear pieces easier to obtain. Marine plywood is almost universally available, unlike clear bending stock. Epoxy and Dynel sheathing fabric can be obtained through mail order.

I want to convince you that you can build this boat, but I don't want to mislead you into thinking that it will be a piece of cake from start to finish. I get phone calls from potential builders telling me that they have just finished a strip canoe, and they are ready to try something a little bigger. Before I sell them a set of plans, I make sure that they understand that although Ocean Pointer may be only a few feet longer than their canoe, in terms of volume and weight it is about ten times greater. The amount of time and money spent can be expected to increase by the same order of magnitude.

If you can realistically find the time and money, building Ocean Pointer will be a rewarding experience. If you are not in a hurry to go fishing, building time can be looked upon as recreation in itself. I believe that this is why most amateurs build their own boats. Looking at it this way, building Ocean Pointer should be ten times as much fun as building that strip canoe! How long should it take to build one for yourself? It takes me, a professional builder, about six hundred man-hours to build a fancy one. If you take your time, the project should give close to a thousand hours of enjoyment.

If lack of experience has you worried, keep in mind what designer/boatbuilder Capt. Pete Culler once said—that "experience starts when you begin." I'll add that experience doesn't stop till you die. I think of myself as a knowledgeable boatbuilder, and yet there is hardly a day that goes by when I don't learn something new. Experience grows as you work. The ability to start a project and see it through to completion in an organized fashion is more important than having a complete knowledge of the trade. Personally, it has been one of life's biggest challenges.

If you think of the entire project at once, building Ocean Pointer may seem daunting. In this book, the project has been divided into a number of small, manageable segments. If each of these segments is taken as a project in itself, you will be less likely to get bogged down. At the beginning of each chapter there is a materials list for that stage of construction. This will help you to plan purchases as you go, so you won't have to buy all the materials at the beginning. Getting started is always the hardest part. After that, you should find that everything will fall into place as you go. Happy Building!

Chapter I
Design and Performance

EVERY TIME I DRIVE PAST a local marina I am astounded at the number of gross plastic gas guzzlers that lie dormant for the winter beneath acres of blue shrink-wrapping. WASTE is written across scores of transoms in capital letters—the epitome of Western Civilization. Warning lights are flashing, telling me I'd better be careful here. Perhaps you are the proud owner of one of these vessels, but no offense is intended. If you read on, you'll see that I am only trying to make a point.

This is not an aesthetic judgment. In my German dictionary, "gross" means "large," and I've been told that the colloquial use of the term originated from describing a person as being "gross" if their presence or ego was too big and overbearing. The term has evolved to mean yucky or stomach turning, which is not my intention when talking about boats that might be owned by some of my readers. I only mean that many modern powerboats have an interior volume that is larger than needed for such a short waterline length, and that huge hull volume combined with fiberglass construction creates a very heavy boat. Add a deep-V bottom section to this equation, and you have a vessel that will need a sinful amount of power to get up and plane—hence the gas guzzling. I am appalled when I see a 23-foot boat with 400 horses slung from the stern. Fuel consumption for such a craft is about twelve times as much as that of a Pointer with a 50-horsepower four-stroke engine.

To vee or not to vee: A question of flat bottom vs. deadrise

In modern powerboat design, two qualities are, in my opinion, overrated. One is the ability to jump big waves at high speed, and the other is full standing headroom. If today's boat owners knew the true cost of these amenities, I'm sure that many would be willing to look carefully at other options.

Wave-jumping at high speed requires a hull form commonly known as a deep-V if the passengers are not to be reduced to a pulp by the pounding. The term deep-V refers to the angle of the bottom between the keel and chine, viewed in cross section. This angle is called deadrise; a flat-bottomed boat has 0 degrees of deadrise, where a deep-V hull might have a deadrise of 16 degrees or more. Many designers and buyers of powerboats are taken in by the obvious advantages of adding deadrise to soften the ride without seeing the disadvantages that grow as the deadrise angle increases. For any given hull size and weight, increased deadrise requires a significant increase in engine horsepower if the boat is to plane. Other disadvantages include decreased stability, especially at high speed, uncomfortable rolling motion in a beam sea, chine-walking (more about that later), and increased draft.

Headroom is seen as indispensable, and yet most time below decks is spent sitting or lying down. When standing headroom is squeezed into a small boat, topsides have to be made too high, and cabin trunks become tall and boxy, adding windage and further increasing the boat's appetite for power.

In a planing hull, weight and bottom shape are two major factors that govern planing ability, and the speed that can be attained for a given horsepower. A planing boat uses what engineers call dynamic lift to free itself from the wavemaking drag that limits the speed of a heavy-displacement-type hull. As a planing hull moves through the water, the hull forces the water downward. Since for every action there is an equal and opposite reaction, the boat is lifted upward with a pressure that equals the downward force. If you picture how a water ski works, the principle is easy to grasp. As I understand it, a boat with a flat bottom will plane the most easily because the water is being deflected nearly straight downward. A deep-V hull, on the other hand, will not plane as easily because much energy is wasted by sideways deflection of the water as the hull moves through the water. When we talk about weight as a factor for planing ability, we actually mean weight versus planing surface. Think of the water ski once more, easily carrying a 150-pound person, and then think how much harder it would be for the same ski to carry three people. Imagine the ski with a V-bottom and three people aboard, and you'll have a good analogy for today's power cruiser. It is only by sheer horsepower that these boats are able to get out of their own way. When you go to buy the motor and keep the fuel tank full, that horsepower translates directly into dollars and cents.

After criticizing the deep-V concept, let me say that in some cases it is the only hull shape that makes sense. Sport fishermen who plan to go offshore and need to get out and back in a hurry

- **To vee or not to vee: A question of flat bottom vs. deadrise**
- **Ocean Pointer's hull lines, and how they affect performance**

regardless of conditions need a boat of this type. For certain uses the extra cost of owning a deep-V hull can be justified. It bothers me, though, that so many boaters think they need a deep-V simply because the power is available, and gas is relatively cheap. Many people would be better served by a lighter boat with a flat or nearly flat bottom. The only difference with the lighter boat is that when the going gets rough, one has to slow down to displacement or semi-planing speeds until the comfort level is within reason. This is a small price to pay in the balance between economy and performance.

In every boat design, a compromise must be found between a number of opposing factors for the boat to best fulfill its intended purpose. If one quality is to be favored, then others will be compromised. In the Pointer-style hull, we have given up the ability to blast through big seas at breakneck speed, and we have lost the four berths, dinette, enclosed head, and unfortunately, the jacuzzi. What we are left with is an honest, unimposing, undemanding, and trustworthy little vessel. She will show a good turn of speed with low horsepower, which means that she won't cost much to run, and you will be surprised at how comfortable and dry she is in a chop. Handling at speed is excellent, and she doesn't share her deep-V counterpart's nasty habit of chine-walking: As a deep-V boat goes faster, the hull rises farther and farther out of the water until at some point the waterline width becomes too narrow to support the boat in a level fashion. At this point the boat suddenly falls over onto one chine, often with little warning. The only cure is a quick response in reducing throttle. The waterline of a Pointer-style boat maintains most of its width as speed is increased, giving a much more stable ride.

I'll make one more comparison before putting the deep-V subject to rest. For every planing boat, there is a transition zone where the boat is beginning to exceed its hull speed in the displacement mode, but it is not yet planing fully. For a deep-V hull, especially one with a wide beam at the waterline, this transition can be awkward as the boat tends to dig a deep hole in the water that it needs to climb out of. Handling is generally very poor in this "semi-planing" mode. A Pointer, on the other hand, has a relatively narrow waterline beam and soft bilges so that she easily and gradually comes up on the plane with little fuss during the transition. Powerboat wakes are a big issue in many places. In harbors and narrow waterways, a heavy deep-V craft will have to slow down to a crawl to avoid making an unpleasant wake. A relatively narrow, light, low-deadrise craft such as the Pointer will rarely generate much wake at any speed. Ironically, then, in places where wakes are regulated, a slower boat becomes the faster boat.

Ocean Pointer's hull lines, and how they affect performance

Every shape, curve, and dimension of a boat's hull has an effect on performance. When I was designing Ocean Pointer, there were a number of factors that needed to be considered in order to achieve the best balance of qualities for the boat's intended use. Although I was following the general dimensions and style of Alton Wallace's West Pointer, there were an infinite number of possible variations in hull form within those parameters. The lines for the finished design can be seen in Figure 1. For purposes of comparison, the lines of Wallace's 18-footer are also shown, courtesy of The Apprenticeshop of Rockland (Figure 2).

Let's take a look at some of the opposing factors that had to be balanced as the model for Ocean Pointer took shape.

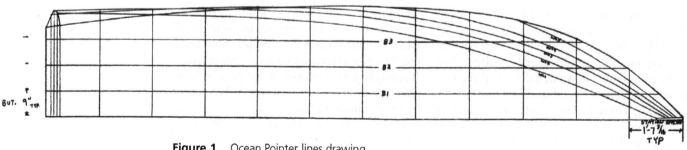

Figure 1 Ocean Pointer lines drawing

For any boat, power or sail, length generally translates directly into comfort. The longer the boat, the less it will be affected by waves. No matter how well it is designed and built, a short boat will pitch and pound more than a longer one. For a small outboard boat such as the Pointer, every foot added to the length will add appreciably to the comfort of the ride. The balancing factors are cost, weight, and handling in tight turns. It is easy to see why adding length will add to the cost and weight. As for the handling, it seems that for planing hulls, a length-to-beam ratio at the waterline is best at about 3 to 1; any less, and the boat makes a "footprint" on the water that is long and narrow, which resists turning. I have seen successful designs for planing boats with lower beam-to-length ratios, but their designers had knowledge and experience that I do not, as yet, possess. To keep the building and operating costs within reason, and to avoid tempting fate, I opted to keep the ratio at approximately 3 to 1 on Ocean Pointer. She is a little longer in proportion to beam than West Pointer.

On the subject of waterline "footprints," there is another important factor that greatly influences handling. I've been told that for best handling in turns, a planing boat should have its widest waterline beam at the transom. Viewed from above, the waterline should be wedge-shaped, and although it may stay the same width some distance forward from the transom, it should never be narrower at the transom than it is amidships. At planing speed, not much of the hull is in the water, and bearing surface is needed aft. If the hull width were to diminish towards the stern, bearing surface would be lost, and the water rushing past the hull would create suction, causing the boat to squat. Having the waterline wide at the stern makes sense anyway for an outboard boat, as it is there that buoyancy is most needed to support the motor(s).

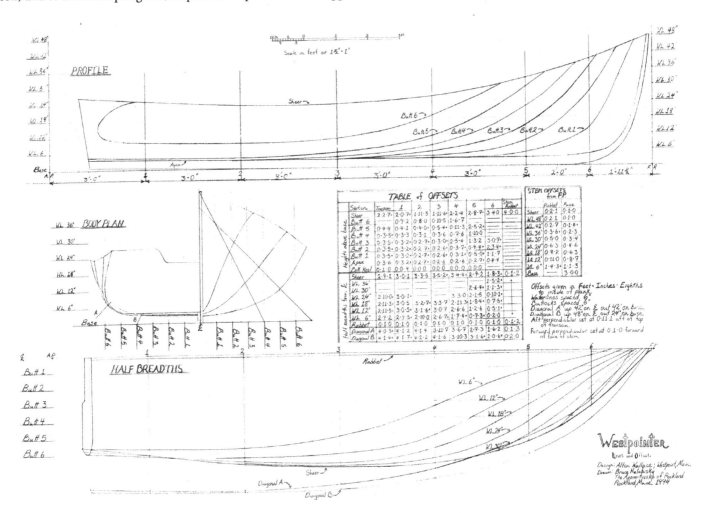

Figure 2 Lines of Wallace 18-footer, courtesy of The Apprenticeshop of Rockland

The shape of the bottom in profile is also important. Viewed from the side, the bottom of a low-speed displacement hull should have a certain amount of "rocker," or curvature, with the bottom of the transom coming clear of the water or nearly so. This allows the water to flow smoothly past the stern keeping turbulence and drag to a minimum. A planing boat, on the other hand, should have its transom immersed so that the bottom profile is straight, or nearly so. This gives the hull its necessary planing surface, which lifts the boat when power is applied. Too much rocker will create suction as the speed increases so that the boat will "dig a hole" in the water instead of getting up and planing.

While the profile aft is important for planing, the underwater profile forward affects handling. There is a touchy balance between too much depth of forefoot, and too little. Too much forefoot can be dangerous in a following sea, as it can dig into the back of a wave and cause the boat's stern to swing around violently, an action known as broaching-to. Broaching can lead to capsize if the conditions are bad enough. However, if the boat has too little forefoot, she will not turn easily at low speed, and only slide sideways when the helm is put over. For good response at low speed, a certain amount of lateral resistance is needed forward to offset the turning moment given by the motor at the stern. In Ocean Pointer, for ease of building I kept the depth of the hull parallel to the waterline from transom to forefoot, and added an exterior forefoot of oak about 2½ inches deep. After trying out the finished boat in a variety of conditions, I'd say that this is just the right amount of forefoot for the design.

A certain amount of freeboard (height of sides) is good, but it is easy to overdo, especially when headroom is a priority. Since Ocean Pointer is designed as a day boat, and not an overnighter, extra topside height becomes less important. I gave the model enough freeboard to keep green water from coming aboard in any conditions that the boat was likely to encounter. Anything more would have done little except to increase wind resistance and needed horsepower. The sleek profile looks good to my eye, a factor that I try not to ignore in any design.

The only functional difference between Ocean Pointer and West Pointer is that Ocean Pointer is longer (while keeping about the same beam), and she has fuller sections forward below the waterline. This was done more from intuition than from understanding, but as it turned out, the lower angle of deadrise in the forward sections helped to give Ocean Pointer a drier ride. The spray gets diverted sideways rather than climbing the sides. You would think she would pound more, but the extra length seems to help in this regard so that the ride is comfortable as well as dry.

In summary, the two major factors that make the Pointer-style hull successful are light weight and a flat bottom for easy planing. Soft bilges and an easy entry soften the ride. Please don't spoil your Ocean Pointer by raising the topsides, adding cabins, or otherwise increasing weight and windage. If you keep her pure and simple, the benefits of the type will not be lost.

Chapter II
Getting Started

A LITTLE ADVANCE PLANNING will go a long way towards helping the job go smoothly and easily.

- Setting up your shop
- A building platform
- Tools
- Lighting
- Pencils
- Heat
- Safe use of power tools
- Safe handling of epoxy
- Tips for successful gluing
- Construction overview
- Materials and supplies

Setting up your shop
For a workspace, you will need a minimum of 13 feet of width, 24 feet long. It will be handy to have on each side of the building area a narrow workbench made out of a 16-foot 2 x 12. These benches will be useful when it comes time to bevel the strips while planking the hull.

A building platform
Ocean Pointer will be built upside down, and this requires a flat, level surface on which to set up the molds. If your shop is blessed with a flat, level wooden floor, the molds can be set up directly on the floor. Otherwise, you will need to build a platform of some sort. How you accomplish this will vary according to what kind of floor your shop has. A simple ladder frame will work in most situations. Set up two straight 20-foot 2 x 4s on edge 4 feet apart, leveled across and lengthwise, with a 2 x 4 cross piece at every other mold location or station. If your floor is concrete or wood, a few cedar shingles should be sufficient to shim the ladder frame level. If you have a dirt floor, 1 x 3 stakes driven into the ground at 3-foot intervals will serve as a foundation for the longitudinal 2 x 4s. A piece of heavy nylon string and a string level are useful in setting up the ladder frame.

Tools

Stationary Power Tools

A 12-inch (or larger) bandsaw and a 10-inch tablesaw are almost indispensable. A 12-inch (or larger) thickness planer would be very useful. You'll want a bench grinder for sharpening tools, also. A small bench-model drill press is great for making bungs using Fuller plug cutters. These are available from Hamilton Marine, The WoodenBoat Store, and Jamestown Distributors (see Appendix I).

Hand-held Power Tools
In the "extremely useful" category, I would suggest:

Two cordless drills with extra batteries, an assortment of Fuller taper drills with "type C" countersinks, and power screwdriver bits of sizes 8 through 14 — all are available from the above-named suppliers

Sabersaw with coarse and fine wood-cutting blades

10-inch circular saw with carbide combination blade

Slow-turning (3,000 rpm or less) circular sander with 8-inch soft pad (Norton or 3M)

3¼-inch hand-held electric plane

4-inch angle grinder with 50- and 80-grit discs

5-inch random-orbit sander with 120- to 220-grit discs

Hand Tools

A complete set of ordinary carpentry tools is essential. A set of diamond sharpening stones, coarse and fine, is high on the list. It is most important to know how to sharpen tools to a razor edge, and to keep them that way. Working wood with a sharp tool is a joy. With a dull tool, frustration is inevitable. If you sharpen frequently, a few swipes on the stone will restore the edge, but if you let a tool get really dull, it will take a while to get it sharp again.

A low-angle block plane will see a lot of use, and a rabbet plane is handy but not essential. If you are planning to varnish the transom, coamings, etc., a cabinet scraper will work well to remove any swirls left by the power sander.

Lighting

In addition to any permanent lighting and windows in the shop, it is nice to have a few clamp lamps to use where extra illumination is needed. These are especially useful when fairing and painting the hull. It's nice to have a light source down low, at about belt height, to bring out any unfair places on the hull.

Pencils

Pencils—how many hundreds of hours have I wasted in search of these wayward creatures. Somewhere in the universe, there must be a black hole that is chock full of them. One time, as an experiment, my brother and I bought a gross of pencils and cast the whole batch in handfuls around the shop. Things were great, for a while. Any time you needed a pencil, there would be one within arm's length. Within three or four months, though, there was nary a pencil to be seen. Lately, I have been using mechanical pencils with 0.7mm lead. They never need sharpening, and for some reason I seem to be able to keep track of them better.

Heat

In colder climates you'll need a heat source to keep the shop warm while the epoxy cures. If you are working in an unheated space, you can decrease the curing time by draping a plastic tent over the work with a small electric heater inside. Heat lamps work well if they are aimed directly at smaller glue jobs. Don't leave heat sources unattended for any length of time. I'm not your mother, and I'm not afraid of liability. I tell you this because of personal experiences with fire.

Once, while welding I accidentally set fire to a pile of oil-soaked wood chips that hadn't been cleaned up from under the planer. My planer is one of those cast-iron monsters from around the turn of the century. It has Babbit bearings that need to be oiled before each use, and an accumulation of oil spills had provided a good fuel supply for the fire. By the time I had filled a couple of buckets of water and extinguished the blaze, the shop was full of acrid smoke as thick as Maine fog. Another time I set fire to a pile of old tires that were too close to my wood-fired steambox. I was subcontracting at a marina and didn't have any liability insurance. The last thing I wanted to do is burn down their sheds. The foreman ran to the scene and deployed the nearest fire extinguisher (it looked to be about the same vintage as my planer) which fanned the flames with a nice blast of fresh air before expiring with a final gasp. Fortunately we were able to send smoke signals to the fire department, and the blaze was extinguished. The one real loss I have experienced by fire was not my fault. My first boatshop was leveled by the work of an arsonist, who hit several other unoccupied buildings the same night.

I don't lie awake at night worrying about fire, but I am more careful than I used to be. I still leave shavings under the planer, but the welder has been banished to outdoors. I am fastidious about not leaving oily rags around, and am very careful about woodstove installation and use.

Safe use of power tools

Building the Ocean Pointer requires the use of several stationary and hand-held power tools. I am assuming that you know how to operate these tools safely. If you are inexperienced with the use of power tools, get someone knowledgeable to show you how to use them safely.

Safe use of power tools is as much a matter of attitude as it is of knowledge. You must never lose respect for machinery, no matter how long you've been using it. I've known a number of woodworkers who were injured while using power tools. None of them were novices. Over the years, they had lost their fear and were too comfortable with the machines they were using. Don't be in a hurry, and always move slowly and deliberately. A split second of inattention, and, whoops—where'd those fingers go?

This is not a manual on shop safety. But I so often have been appalled at the risks taken by table saw operators, I feel a duty to point out a few basic safety principles. Most of the table saw accidents I've been aware of occurred because the operator reached across to the back of the saw to retrieve the piece that had been pushed through. You will never see me reach across the saw. It takes a little more effort to walk around to the back of the saw and pick up the piece off of the floor, but a little exercise never hurts. A few rules for safe use of the table saw:

1. Don't let your hands or any part of your body get behind the blade. A long push-stick will get the piece through the saw safely.

2. Don't put short pieces through the table saw. They are more likely to kick back.

3. Don't use the fence when cross-cutting. Use the miter guide.

4. Don't be in a hurry. (Think of how much time the saw is saving—what's a few more seconds to do the job safely?)

5. Keep blades sharp. A dull blade is more likely to kick back.

Even without power tools, boatbuilding can be hazardous. When I mentioned life-extending petrochemicals in the Introduction, I was referring to the life of the boat. Unfortunately, exposure to the same compounds can have the opposite effect on the life of the builder. The air in a modern boatshop can become poisonous with fine sawdust, and fumes from solvents, paints, and adhesives. Good ventilation and a charcoal respirator are needed when these hazards are present.

Safe handling of epoxy

Again, this is not a comprehensive guide, but here are a few special precautions regarding the safe handling of epoxy:

First, avoid mixing it in large batches. The bigger the batch, the faster it heats up in the mixing tub. We've actually had epoxy start to smoke, and then burst into flames from mixing too big a batch. The smoke is noxious, so don't breathe it. If your pot of glue starts to smoke, do as I do—hold your breath, run to the door, and drop-kick it into the driveway. If you do need to mix up more than a half pint at a time, you can slow the curing reaction by pouring the resin into a wide, shallow pan. The extra surface area will help to keep the resin cool.

Exposure to epoxy can cause skin sensitization. Once you become sensitized, you won't be able to get near the stuff without breaking out in a rash. To avoid this fate, observe the following precautions:

1. Keep uncured epoxy off your skin. To avoid getting uncured epoxy in your pores, use a combination of protective skin cream and vinyl gloves. Latex gloves have been known to cause skin rashes. I had an employee who blamed his rash on exposure to epoxy. The actual cause was the latex gloves that we used to keep epoxy off our hands!

2. Wear a charcoal respirator any time the shop smells of fumes from curing epoxy.

3. Especially avoid breathing the dust created from sanding green (partially cured) epoxy. Breathing this dust is much worse than breathing the vapors, because the partially cured epoxy sits in your lungs and poisons you for a long period of time, whereas the vapors are cleared out quickly with a little fresh air. Epoxy can be considered "green" for two weeks after the initial cure.

4. If you get uncured epoxy on your skin, it can be washed off with white vinegar. This is much better for your skin than acetone or denatured alcohol.

Tips for successful gluing

To ensure the best bonding with epoxy glue, use the following procedures:

1. The surfaces to be bonded should be clean, dry, and newly planed or sanded. A few days in the sunlight can break down the fibers on the surface of the wood, creating an inferior bond.

2. Unthickened epoxy penetrates well, but it is not very strong. To achieve the best joint, paint unthickened epoxy on both surfaces, and after the epoxy has had time to soak in for a few minutes, goop one of the surfaces with epoxy thickened with cotton fibers or colloidal silica before clamping the two pieces together. Priming with unthickened epoxy is especially recommended for cases where end-grain is involved. Otherwise, a "dry joint" may occur when the end-grain drinks all the resin out of the glue, possibly causing the joint to fail.

3. Don't clamp the joint too tightly. It will be stronger if some of the epoxy is left in the joint.

4. Follow the directions on the can for temperature conditions. The dispensing pumps for epoxy resin will not work well if the resin is cooler than 60 degrees.

5. You may find it worth your while to store your epoxy in a homemade "incubator." All you need is a box made of Styrofoam insulation board with a lightbulb inside to keep the resin at a workable viscosity.

6. You can save a lot of sanding and scraping time if you work neatly and clean up excess epoxy before it cures. Wood that will be finished bright can be wiped clean with a rag soaked in alcohol.

7. In spite of careful wiping, there will be some drips and runs in the cured epoxy that must be planed or chiseled. This job will be much easier if done while the glue is still leathery—usually two to six hours after the initial cure. Don't wait until the glue is rock-hard, or you'll have a job to plane it off.

How to Build
The Ocean Pointer

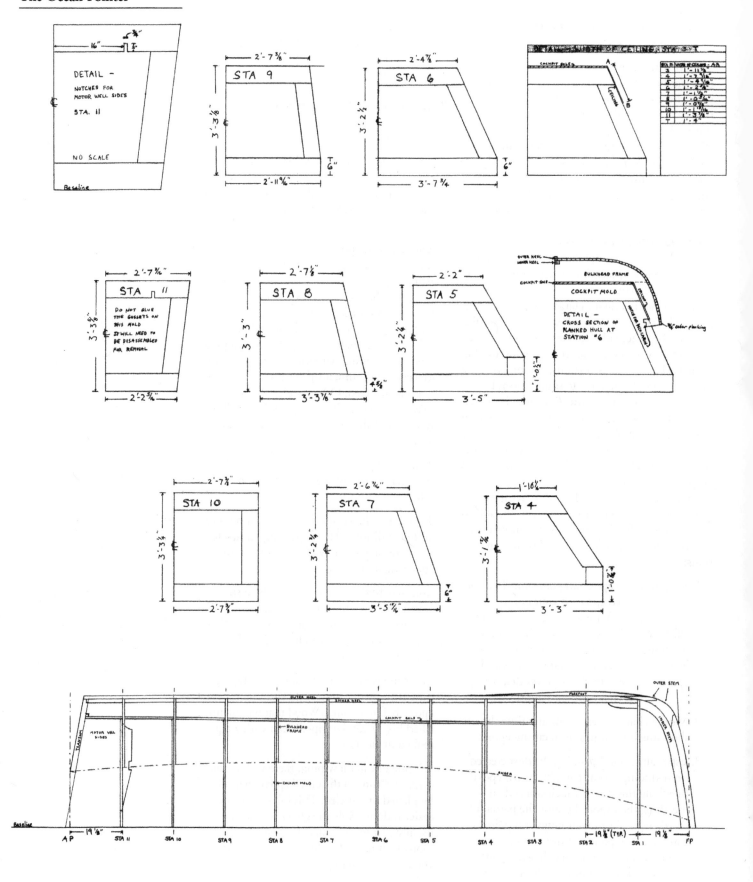

Figure 3 Sheet 2 of the plans

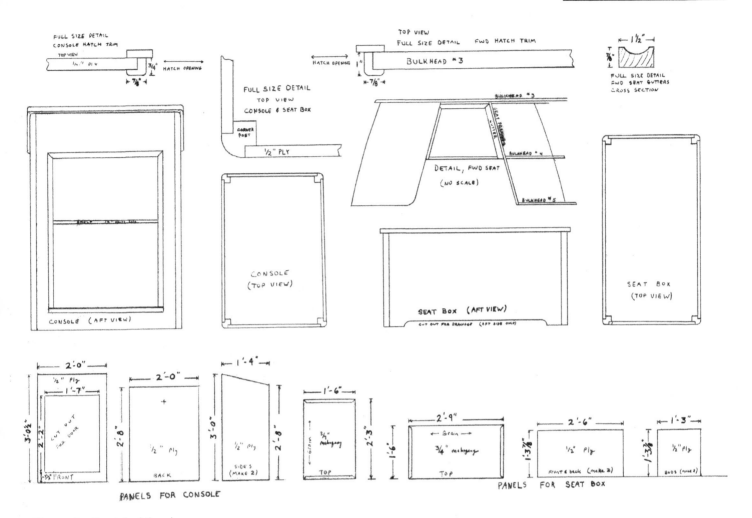

Figure 4 Sheet 3 of the plans

Construction overview

Here is an overview of the basic construction sequence. If you take the time to read and understand this, you'll be able to make more sense out of the detailed step-by-step instructions that follow (see Figures 3 and 5).

Construction of the Ocean Pointer is unusual in that the cockpit is built first, before the hull is framed and planked. Molds for the cockpit are built and set up on a flat, level surface, according to the dimensions given on Sheet 2, and then the transom, motorwell sides, and bulkhead No. 3 are installed. Next, the cockpit sole and sides are installed. Bulkhead frames are then cut out and installed around the outside of the cockpit. The keel is then glued into notches in the bulkhead frames, and the laminated stem is fastened to the keel. The bulkhead frames are beveled, and the bevel on the stem is checked with a batten. The outer keel is installed, and Styrofoam flotation is glued to the outside of the cockpit.

The hull is now ready to plank. Cedar strips are milled out, beveled, edge-glued and nailed to each other, and nailed to the bulkhead frames; a fillet of epoxy bonds the planking to the bulkhead frames. The outer stem and forefoot are fitted and fastened, and the hull is then faired, sanded, undercoated, and flipped right-side up.

After the sheer is faired, the deck framing is installed, inner rubrails are fitted and fastened, and the plywood deck is laid. The deck and cockpit are then sheathed with Dynel fabric and epoxy. Coamings and outer rubrails are installed, seats and console are built and installed, and spray rails are fitted. The boat is now ready for paint, varnish, hardware, and controls.

1. Make and set up cockpit molds
2. Set up forward bulkheads and inner stem
3. Set up sides of motorwell
4. Install cockpit sole over cockpit molds
5. Install ceiling over cockpit molds
6. Install transom on motorwell sides
7. Install bulkhead frames around cockpit
8. Plank and fair hull
9. Install outer stem and forefoot
10. Remove from molds and flip hull

Materials and supplies

In the chapters that follow we have broken the building sequence into several stages. At the beginning of each chapter, there is a list of materials necessary to complete that particular stage of construction. These materials lists will be especially helpful if you are not planning to buy all the materials before you start building. Use the lists to plan your materials purchases as you go along. Avoid ordering materials at the last minute—it can be very frustrating if the whole job is held up for lack of a few fastenings. If your budget won't allow you to buy all the materials in the beginning, plan a purchasing schedule that will help you to buy supplies while keeping pace with your rate of progress.

Retail prices for marine paints and adhesives, fastenings, and hardware are very high. Discount mail-order sources for these items can be found in Appendix I.

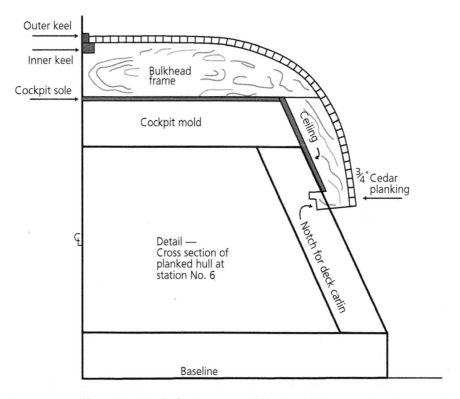

Figure 5 Detail of cross-section of planked hull at station No. 6

Chapter III
Making Molds and Patterns

Materials

Full-sized pattern sheets (available from Stimson Marine—see Appendix I)

Molds—24 pieces #3 pine ¾ inch by 6 inches, 8 feet long; or three sheets ¾-inch C/D plywood

Gussets—24 lineal feet ½-inch plywood, cut in strips 5 inches wide

Pattern stock—three sheets ¼-inch lauan plywood

Fastenings—2 pounds 1¼-inch sheetrock screws

Two cans spray adhesive

Yellow carpenter's glue

Making the cockpit molds

Figure 3 (Sheet 2 in the blueprints) shows the dimensions for the eight cockpit molds. These can be made from 1 x 6-inch pine or ¾-inch C/D plywood. If you are using plywood, you may set the table saw fence to 5⅞ inches to allow for the saw kerf, to make the best use of the material.

You'll need a flat surface, about 4 feet x 8 feet, to lay out and assemble the molds. A sheet of ½-inch A/C plywood will suffice if your shop floor is not suitable. First, draw an 8-foot horizontal baseline a few inches from one edge of the plywood. This will serve as a reference line for laying out the cockpit molds. All of the vertical dimensions for the cockpit molds will be measured from this line.

Now draw a 4-foot-long vertical line square to the baseline in the center of the baseline. This vertical line represents the centerline of each mold. All of the horizontal dimensions will be measured from this line.

Using the dimensions from Sheet 2, lay out the shape of the first mold on the floor, using the baseline and centerline as guides. Begin by cutting out the piece that goes across the bottom of the mold, and screw it to the plywood on the baseline with a couple of sheetrock screws. Make the uprights next, and screw them to the plywood. Then cut and fasten down the top crosspiece.

Get out the ½-inch plywood gusset stock, and make enough gussets to lap several inches across each joint in the mold. Then, glue and screw the gussets to the mold using carpenter's glue and 1¼-inch sheetrock screws. Don't forget to mark the centerline on the mold, top and bottom. Now you can mark the station number on the mold with a magic marker, and unscrew it from the floor. Repeat this procedure until you have made all eight molds. Put mold No. 11 together without glue; it will have to be disassembled before the boat is taken off the form.

Patternmaking

Full-sized patterns are included for the bulkhead frames, transom, inner and outer stem, forefoot, and motorwell sides. You will want to transfer these patterns onto ¼-inch plywood. Tape the paper pattern onto the plywood, and make a series of prick marks on the lines to transfer the shape onto the plywood. Or, if you don't mind the extra expense and the smell, stick the paper onto the plywood with spray adhesive, available in most hardware stores. I have used 3M and Elmer's; there may be other brands. Cut out the patterns with a sabersaw, using a fine-toothed blade. Take your time to do a nice job when you make the patterns. Accuracy in patternmaking will minimize cumulative errors that can slow your progress when it comes time to fair the bulkhead frames.

Note: some of the patterns are actually half-patterns. One edge of a half-pattern will be the centerline of the actual piece. Look for the CL mark on the centerline of these patterns.

- **Materials**
- **Making the cockpit molds**
- **Patternmaking**

How to Build
The Ocean Pointer

Chapter IV

The Backbone: Keel, Stem, and Transom

Materials

Inner keel—oak, mahogany, yellow pine, or Douglas-fir, 1¼ inches by 3¾ inches, 19 feet long

Outer keel—oak, mahogany, yellow pine, or Douglas-fir, 1¼ inches by 2 inches, 19 feet long

Laminated inner stem—12 pieces oak bending stock ¼ inch by 2⅝ inches, 6 feet long; or 24 pieces ⅛-inch mahogany, fir, or yellow pine

Laminating jig for inner stem—one sheet ½-inch C/D plywood or 7/16-inch waferboard

Outer stem—oak, mahogany, fir or yellow pine, one piece 3 inches by 3¼ inches by 3 feet 6 inches long; one piece 2 inches by 3 inches by 2 feet long; one piece 3 inches by 6 inches by 1 foot 6 inches long; may be laminated

Forefoot—oak, mahogany, fir, or yellow pine, 2 inches by 3 inches, 5 feet long; may be laminated

Transom—two 4-by-8-foot sheets ⅝-inch marine plywood, and four mahogany or oak boards ¾ inch by 8 inches by 6 feet long (save the excess plywood for the cockpit sole)

Five gallons epoxy resin and fillers (this will give you enough to complete the planking and woodwork)

Fastenings—150 #10 flathead bronze wood screws, 1 inch long

Inner and outer keel

If you have trouble getting a 19-foot piece for the inner keel, you can make it out of two pieces, scarfed together. Use a 12-to-1 scarf joint glued with epoxy. Do the gluing on a long, flat workbench where you can snap a straight chalkline to line up the keel.

Joints become slippery when coated with wet epoxy. Alignment of the joint will be easier if you drill holes for three or four #10 screws while the scarf is clamped to the bench for a "dry run" before the epoxy is applied. After you have gooped up the scarf joint, screw it down to the bench with #10, 2-inch screws. The pre-drilled holes will line up the joint and keep it from slipping when you put the screws in. (Don't forget to put a piece of plastic or waxed paper under the joint so you won't glue the keel to the bench.)

The outer keel may also be scarfed if necessary. Stagger the joints of the inner and outer keels so that they will not be in the same fore-and-aft locations.

- Materials
- Inner and outer keel
- The inner stem
- The outer stem
- The forefoot
- The transom

Photo 1 The bending jig

How to Build The Ocean Pointer

Photo 2   Gooping the stem laminations

Photo 3   Clamping the laminations to the jig

The inner stem

The inner stem will be laminated over a jig. For the stem laminations, you'll need strips 2⅝ inches wide by 6 feet long. If you are using good-quality bending oak, the stem can be made from twelve layers of ¼-inch stock. Mahogany, fir, and yellow pine will not bend as well as oak, so you'll need to go to 3/16 inch or ⅛ inch for the laminations. Make enough pieces to give a total thickness of 3 inches.

The bending jig for the inner stem (Photo 1) will be built up out of several layers of plywood or waferboard, stacked and screwed together. Some carpenter's glue between the layers wouldn't hurt. Use the pattern from Sheet 7 to lay out the shape of the jig on the plywood. If you are using ½-inch ply, you'll need five layers. The 7/16-inch waferboard will require six layers.

Laminating the stem can be messy, so wear old clothes or coveralls. I have too many work clothes because I thought I wouldn't get any goop on me. Clamp the jig in a vise, and have eight or ten 8-inch or larger C-clamps or sliding bar clamps ready. Staple some plastic to the outer surface of the jig, or cover it with a layer of duct tape so that you won't glue the stem to the jig. Then screw four or five blocks to one side of the jig to help keep the laminations lined up. These blocks should also be covered with duct tape (see Photo 1). Mix up a batch of epoxy, and coat the laminations, stacking them as you go (Photo 2). Then grab the whole slippery bundle, line up the ends, and clamp one end of the whole bundle to the jig (Photo 3). A crossways clamp with a wooden pad underneath will help to keep the layers lined up. Slowly bend the bundle of laminations around the jig, clamping it down and crossways, until it is held securely to the jig with no voids (Photos 4 and 5). Then scrape off the excess uncured glue. This is much easier than chiseling or planing it off after it has cured.

After the epoxy has cured, remove the stem from the jig (Photo 6), and plane off any glue that didn't get wiped off. Lay the pattern onto the stem (Photo 7) and tack it down. Trace the outline of the pattern onto the stem, remove the pattern, and cut the stem to shape on the bandsaw. Tack the pattern back onto the stem and drive a series of tacks along the beveling line on the pattern to transfer that line onto the stem (Photo 7). Then, mark the beveling line on the opposite side of the stem using the same nail holes in the pattern as a guide.

The Backbone: Keel, Stem, and Transom

The sides of the stem will be beveled to give the planking a flat surface to land on. You've just marked the beveling line on the sides. Now you'll need to mark the lines on the forward face of the stem. Use the pattern on the pattern sheet to lay out this line. You can stick the pattern directly to the face of the stem using spray adhesive.

Now you are ready to bevel the stem. The stem will not be beveled all the way to the top; you will be ending the bevel at the sheerline. First, make a cut on the sheer mark with a handsaw, cutting down to the beveling lines on each side. Then plane the bevels on both sides of the stem to the beveling lines from the sheer to the bottom of the stem.

The outer stem

Cut out the three pieces for the outer stem to the profile shown on the pattern sheet (Photo 8); leave a little extra wood to allow for fitting. Then mark a centerline along the inner and outer faces. Set the outer stem aside. You will be doing the final fitting after the bulkhead frames, keel, and inner stem are set up.

The forefoot

Cut out the forefoot to the profile given on the pattern sheet. Leave some extra wood for fitting on this piece also. Mark the centerline, and set it aside.

Photos 4 & 5 Bending and clamping the laminations to the jig

Photo 6 Removing the inner stem from the jig

How to Build
The Ocean Pointer

Photo 7 Transferring the beveling line onto the sides of the stem

Photo 8 Tracing the outer stem patterns onto the stock

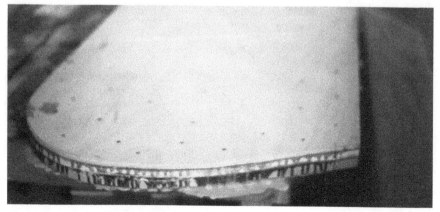

Photo 9 The laminated transom

The transom

The transom will be laminated from two layers of ⅝-inch plywood and one layer of ¾-inch solid mahogany on the outside. Use the pattern for the inside of the transom to mark and cut out the two layers of plywood, leaving about 2 inches of extra wood around the edges. Then joint the edges of the solid mahogany for the outer layer. We found it easiest to glue up the mahogany for the outer layer into a single panel before laminating it to the plywood. Use 1¼-inch flathead screws and a liberal coating of thickened epoxy to fasten the first layer of plywood to the mahogany. You can avoid bunging if you put the screws in from the inside. Don't countersink the screw heads, or the tips of the screws will poke through the mahogany on the outside. Then glue and screw the second layer of plywood to the first (Photo 9).

After the glue has cured, plane and rough-sand the outside of the transom, and draw a vertical centerline inside and out. From the patterns, mark the shape of the outside and inside on the transom. Note that the inside is bigger, except at the top of the transom where it is smaller due to the rake and the shape of the sheer. Lay the transom inside up and, using a sharp sabersaw, cut it out with the saw set square on 0 degrees, except for the top edge, which you will cut square from the outside. This top edge will be beveled to fit the underside of the deck after the boat has been flipped right-side up.

Chapter V
Making the Bulkhead Frames and Setting Up

Materials

Bulkhead frames and motorwell sides—four 4-by-8-foot sheets marine plywood—fir or okoume

Cockpit sole—two sheets ⅝-inch marine plywood (plus the leftover pieces from the transom)

Cleat stock—⅞-by-⅞-inch oak or mahogany, 30 feet long; ⅞-by-⅞-inch oak or mahogany, 6 feet long, ripped with a 10-degree bevel top and bottom

Ceiling—two sheets ¼-inch marine plywood—fir or okoume

Fastenings—100 #10 flathead bronze wood screws, 1½ inches long

Bedding—two cartridges adhesive sealant (such as Sikaflex or 3M 5200)

Fastenings—25 #14 flathead bronze wood screws, 2¼ inches long, for stem and outer keel

Control cable conduits—two pieces 2-inch flexible black polyethylene water pipe, 8 feet long

Flotation—twelve sheets 1½-inch Styrofoam, 24 inches wide by 8 feet long

Adhesive—10 cartridges Styrobond or similar

Bulkhead frames and motorwell sides

From the patterns, trace the shape of the bulkhead frames and motorwell sides onto the ¾-inch plywood. Lay out the larger frames first, and fill in the spaces that are left with the smaller patterns. Lay out all the patterns first before you draw the lines, and try to make the most efficient use of the plywood. Draw the lines lightly at first in case you need to change the placement of some of the patterns. Cut out the bulkhead frames and motorwell sides using a sabersaw set on 0 degrees.

The cockpit sole

Set your Skilsaw to a 10-degree bevel, and cut a bevel on the end of one sheet of ⅝-inch plywood (do this with the finish side up if you are using A/B plywood). The beveled end will go up against the transom, which has a 10-degree rake. Retrieve the two pieces of ⅝-inch plywood that were left over from the transom. From these pieces, cut out two 8-inch-wide strips 8 feet long. Cut the same 10-degree bevel on one end of each of the 8-inch strips. Now, with the Skilsaw set on 0 degree, cut the other full sheet of ⅝-inch plywood to a length of 6 feet. From the piece left over, cut four strips off the end, 5¾ inches wide and 4 feet long. Set these pieces aside.

The transom pattern has marked on it the placement for the ⅞-by-⅞-inch oak cleats that support the cockpit sole and ceiling. The side cleats can be cut out square in section. The bottom cleat should be cut out to a 10-degree bevel for the cockpit sole to land on. Screw the cleats to the inside of the transom, using an adhesive sealant such as Sikaflex or 3M 5200 for bedding.

The aft side of bulkhead No. 3 also has cleats fastened to it for the cockpit sole and ceiling to land on. Mark the position of the cleats from the pattern, and goop and fasten them in the same way you did the transom (Photo 10).

- Materials
- Bulkhead frames and motorwell sides
- The cockpit sole
- The ceiling
- Setting up the molds
- Marking the stations and setting up the cockpit molds
- Installing the motorwell sides and bracing the molds
- Installing the cockpit sole and transom
- Installing the ceiling
- Installing the bulkhead frames
- Installing the inner keel
- Installing the stem
- Applying epoxy fillets
- Installing the outer keel
- Beveling the bulkhead frames
- Beveling the forward end of the inner keel
- Beveling the transom
- Sealing the plywood
- Installing the control cable and wiring conduits
- Installing the Styrofoam flotation

Photo 10 Cleats installed on bulkhead frame No. 3

How to Build The Ocean Pointer

Photo 11 Marking stations and centerline on the building platform

Photo 12 Setting up the molds

Photo 13 Cockpit molds all set up (note notches in mold No. 11)

The ceiling

The ceiling (cockpit sides) can be gotten out of two sheets of ¼-inch marine plywood. For now, rip each sheet longitudinally down the center to make four sheets measuring 2 feet by 8 feet.

Setting up the molds

You will need a flat, level floor or platform to set up the molds on. If your floor is not flat, you can build a ladder frame with two parallel 20-foot 2 x 6s on edge, shimmed straight and level and set 4 feet apart. Nail a series of 2 x 6 crosspieces between the longitudinals—a crosspiece at every other station is okay.

Marking the stations and setting up the cockpit molds

The station spacing is 19⅛ inches. Mark the forward perpendicular a few inches from one end of the platform. Then, mark stations 1 through 11 and the aft perpendicular, all spaced at 19⅛ inches. Square the station marks across the platform and number them with a magic marker. Make a longitudinal centerline down the center of the platform by marking the halfway point on the forward and aft perpendiculars and snapping a chalkline. Then re-mark the centerline with a pencil and straightedge on top of the chalkline (Photo 11).

You are now ready to set up the cockpit molds. These will all be set up on the aft side of the station lines. Line up the centerline on each mold with the centerline on the platform, and screw them down to the platform with 2½-inch sheetrock screws (Photos 12 and 13). These are put in as toe fastenings through the sides of the molds. Check each mold with a level. Any molds that are not level should be shimmed on the low side.

Installing the motorwell sides and bracing the molds

After the cockpit molds are set up and leveled, set up bulkhead frame No. 3 on its cradle with the cleats facing aft. The motorwell sides can now be installed. These butt up to the cockpit mold at station No. 11, and are lined up square to the mold (Photo 14). There are notches in the upper crosspiece on cockpit mold No. 11, offset 16 3/8 inches on center from the centerline of the boat. The motorwell sides will be let into these notches. On the platform, draw two parallel lines 16 inches on either side of the centerline between station No. 11 and the aft perpendicular. Set up the motorwell sides with the top in the notches in mold No. 11, and line up the inside edges of the bottom with the 16-inch lines on the platform. Screw the motorwell sides to the platform with 2-inch sheetrock screws. Then screw the top of the mold into the motorwell sides above the notches. Installing the motorwell sides will automatically brace and plumb mold No. 11. You can use mold No. 11 as a reference point to plumb the other cockpit molds and bulkhead frame No. 3. A temporary 1-by-2-inch batten can be screwed to the sides of the molds to hold them plumb.

Installing the cockpit sole and transom

The motorwell sides serve as a transom mold, holding the transom at the correct height and rake while the boat is being built. Once the motorwell sides have been set up, the cockpit sole and transom can be installed.

Find the 5/8-inch plywood pieces that were set aside for the cockpit sole. The two 4-foot-wide pieces will run down the center of the cockpit, and the narrow strips go on the edges. First, strike a chalkline down the centerline of the two 4-foot-wide pieces, top and bottom. Then set the 4-by-8-foot piece on the cockpit molds with the bevel aft, so that the aft edge lines up with the bottom corners of the motorwell sides. Line up the centerline of the piece with the centerlines on the cockpit molds, and fasten the piece down with temporary sheetrock screws into the molds. You are now ready to hang the transom.

Set the transom up so that the two vertical cleats are outboard of the motorwell sides, and the beveled crosswise cleat bears on the bottom of the cockpit sole. Check to make sure that the centerline on the inside of the transom lines up with the centerline on the bottom of the cockpit sole. Now you can install the transom, gluing and screwing the cockpit sole and motorwell sides to the cleats on the transom (Photo 15).

Photo 14 Motorwell sides installed

Photo 15 Transom and cockpit sole installed

How to Build The Ocean Pointer

Photo 16 Cockpit sole installed and the edge beveled for the ceiling

Photos 17 & 18 Ceiling installed and fastened to cleats

The cockpit sole can now be completed. First, you will need the 4-by-6-foot piece of plywood. It will be screwed to the molds, forward of the 8-foot piece already installed, and the forward end will butt up to bulkhead frame No. 3. The actual length of this piece should be about 5 feet 11 inches. Measure the distance between bulkhead frame No. 3 and the 4-by-8-foot piece of cockpit sole already installed, and cut to length. Tack this piece down temporarily until the rest of the cockpit sole has been fitted and beveled.

The two 8-inch-by-8-foot pieces are next. Tack these to the molds on each side, with the beveled ends butting up to the transom. Now tack the shorter pieces down forward of the others. The cockpit sole should now be overhanging the molds on both sides. It will need to be trimmed to a curve at the sides. The shape of this curve is determined by the edges of the molds. Bend a light batten around the molds beneath the cockpit sole and tack it in place; then trace inside the batten on the cockpit sole. When the pieces are removed, they can be cut to shape with a sabersaw or bandsaw, leaving about ⅛ inch for trimming after the cockpit sole is glued into the boat. Now you can glue the pieces into the boat (Photo 16). Use a 4-inch-wide plywood gusset to back up the crosswise joint. Glue the fore-and-aft joints, but don't install any gussets over these yet.

Installing the ceiling

The edges of the cockpit sole must be beveled before the ceiling can be installed. The easiest way to mark the sole for beveling is to make a saw cut through the edge of the sole above the outboard edge of each mold, using the angle of the mold as a guide. If you then put a nail at the end of each saw cut on the bottom of the sole and bend a batten around the nails, a beveling line will be established.

After you have beveled the edge of the sole, fit the ¼-inch marine plywood ceiling (cockpit sides) to the transom and bulkhead frame No. 3, bending it around the cockpit molds and making a butt joint just forward of station No. 8. Let the ceiling overhang the bottom of the cockpit sole until you have fitted the ends. Then mark and cut the bottom of the ceiling flush with the bottom of the cockpit sole. Sheet 2 has on it a layout for the shape of the top edge of the ceiling, measured from the bottom of the cockpit sole at each station. Lay out the width at each station, connect the marks with a batten, and cut to the line. Then the ceiling can be glued in (Photos 17 and 18).

Installing the bulkhead frames

You are now ready to install the bulkhead frames. Start with frame No. 11, and work your way forward (Photos 19 and 20). Glue the crosspiece to the bottom of the sole on the forward side of the station mark, lining up the centerline of the crosspiece with the centerline of the sole. Then glue the side pieces to the crosspiece and to the ceiling. Use sheetrock screws as temporary toe fastenings while the glue sets. You will need to cut slots in the ceiling for bulkhead frames 4 and 5. These frames include the framing for the forward seat; the slots in the ceiling will allow the seat frame portion of the frame to be slid into the cockpit (Photos 21 through 23).

Stations 1 and 2 can now be set up. They are held to the correct height by molds that are set up on the station lines on the building platform. Fasten stations 1 and 2 to the molds using a couple of plywood cleats and sheetrock screws.

The fore-and-aft seams at the sides of the cockpit sole should now be backed up with plywood gussets between the bulkhead frames.

Installing the inner keel

The inner keel is next. There are notches on the centerline of each bulkhead frame; the inner keel will be glued into these notches so that the outer face of the keel is flush with the edge of the frame. The transom will also be notched, but the notch will not be carried all the way through the aft face of the transom. The transom's plywood inner laminations can be marked for the thickness and width of the keel, and the notch cut out with a sharp chisel. The end of the keel can be beveled 10 degrees, and butted to the inner face of the mahogany layer.

Photos 19 & 20 Installing the bulkhead frames

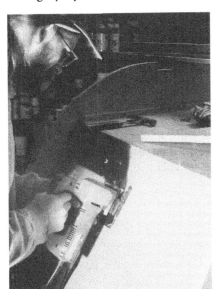
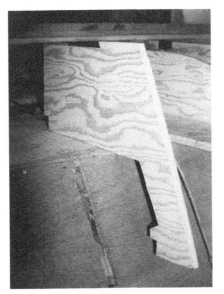
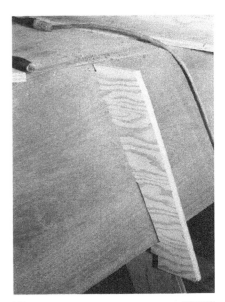

Photos 21–23 Slotting the ceiling for bulkhead frames 4 and 5

Photos 24–26 Inner stem, inner and outer keel, bulkhead frames 1 and 2 installed

Installing the stem

The inner keel will project forward to station No. 1; the heel of the stem will notch around it, and be glued and fastened to it. Line up the forward perpendicular (FP) marks on the sides of the inner stem with the forward perpendicular on the platform, and screw a couple of cleats to the platform and stem to hold it in position. Pull a string down the center of the keel as a guide to make sure the stem is plumb and straight before gluing and fastening it to the keel.

Applying epoxy fillets

The joints between the bulkhead frames and the cockpit sole/ceiling will be stronger if the glue area is increased. Mix up a batch of epoxy and add colloidal silica to make a peanut-butter consistency. Apply a fillet into the corners of all the joints where the bulkhead frames meet the cockpit sole/ceiling. Smooth the fillets with a gloved finger or a tongue depressor.

Installing the outer keel

The outer keel will be installed on the flat on the centerline of the inner keel. The forward end should first be cut to a 10¼-inch-long scarf. Glue and screw the keel down, locating the tip of the scarf on station No. 1 (Photos 24 through 26). Cut off the aft end of the outer keel flush with the outside of the transom. Be sure to clean up any excess epoxy in the rabbet that is formed by the inner and outer keels so the planking will lie flat.

Beveling the bulkhead frames

The bulkhead frames were installed on the forward side of the station marks, which means that their aft faces represent the correct sectional shape of the boat at each station. The frames were cut out at a 90-degree angle. This means that from amidships forward, the frames will need to be beveled so that the planking will lie flat on the edges of the frames; otherwise, the planking will bear only on forward corners of the frames. You can obtain the correct bevels by bending a batten around the frames and shaving the edges of the frames with a spokeshave. You can check the stem bevels with the batten, also, while you are beveling the frames.

Beveling the forward end of the inner keel

The combination of inner and outer keels has formed a 90-degree rabbet. This is the correct angle from the transom forward to station No. 3. From station No. 3 forward, the rabbet becomes a rolling bevel until it fairs into the bevel on the side of the inner stem (Photos 27 and 28). This is most easily accomplished using a sharp rabbet plane. The sides of the outer keel remain plumb until they run out at the scarf at the forward end. Use a batten to check the bevel to make sure the planking will lie flat as it takes the twist from horizontal amidships to nearly vertical at the stem.

Beveling the transom

Earlier, you marked the shape on the outside of the transom from the pattern. Use a batten across the frames as a guide for beveling the edge of the transom to the mark from the keel to the sheer. A spokeshave works well for this.

Sealing the plywood

At this point, all plywood should be sealed before planking begins. Two coats of oil-based polyurethane floor finish are sufficient. Before you begin sealing, mask the edges of the bulkhead frames with 1½-inch masking tape. Wrap the tape over and onto the forward and aft faces of the frames. This will leave about ⅜ inch of bare wood for the epoxy fillets that will help attach the planking to the frames. Avoid sealing the keel rabbet and stem bevel—the adhesive sealants that are used between the backbone and planking will bond better to bare wood.

Photos 27 & 28 Fairing the keel rabbet into the stem bevel

Installing the control cable and wiring conduits

The control cables and wiring harness will be run through two conduits that are installed below the cockpit sole (Photo 29). The conduits are made from two pieces of 2-inch polyethylene water pipe, 8 feet long. They will be installed through holes in bulkhead frames 7 through 11. The locations of these holes are marked on the patterns for the bulkhead frames. Use a 2½-inch hole saw, or a sabersaw, to cut the holes out, then slide the 2-inch water pipes into the holes. Cut them off so that they are overhanging frames 7 and 11 by only a few inches.

Photo 29 Control cable conduits and Styrofoam flotation installed

How to Build
The Ocean Pointer

Photo 30

Installing the Styrofoam flotation

You will be putting two layers of Styrofoam on the bottom of the cockpit sole, and one layer on the sides (Photo 30). Use 1½-inch closed-cell insulation board, available at your local lumberyard. Cut the pieces to the width of each bay on the table saw, or score them with a utility knife and break along the score line. Use Styrofoam adhesive to stick it in place. We get ours in caulking gun–type cartridges from the lumberyard; it is called Styrobond, but there may be other brands. Omit the Styrofoam on the cockpit sides in the aftermost bay, or you will not be able to snake the controls through the conduits.

Chapter VI
Planking

Materials

Planking—2,100 lineal feet Northern or Atlantic white cedar or Eastern white pine, ¾ inch by 1⅜ inches

Fastenings—10 pounds 14-gauge bronze threaded nails, 2½ inches long

Plank-to-keel fastenings—100 #10 flathead bronze wood screws, 1¼ inches long

Bedding—two cartridges adhesive sealant

Removing the temporary fastenings

Before you begin planking, remove the sheetrock screws that fasten the cockpit sole and ceiling to the molds. Otherwise, you will have a difficult time removing the molds after the boat is planked.

Preparing the plank strips

You will need strips 22 feet long for planking the hull. It is unlikely that you'll find clear lumber in such long lengths. Therefore, the strips will need to be joined end-to-end, using either scarfs or finger joints. If scarfed, use 12:1 ratio, which in this case is a 9-inch-long scarf for ¾ inch planking thickness. Glue the joints on a long, straight bench or a flat floor, putting plastic down beneath and between the strips at each joint. Line up the joints as straight as possible so that the planking will go on smoothly.

Planking the hull

The first pair of strips will be bedded and fastened into the rabbet. These will be straight and level from the transom forward to station No. 3. From station No. 3 forward, the planks will take a sharp twist to nearly vertical by the time they cross the inner stem. In order to make the twist without breaking, the first dozen or so planks will need to be "kerfed" on the forward end for about 3 feet. A thin blade on the bandsaw works well for making the saw kerf; hold the plank on edge, and make a cut down the center about 3 feet long.

The edges of the first pair of planks must be beveled from station No. 3 forward in order to make a tight fit against the outer keel. When you are satisfied with the fit, goop the entire rabbet with adhesive sealant, and work some thickened epoxy into the kerf in the forward end of the plank. Then clamp the plank into place, and edge-nail it to the outer keel. Twist the forward end into position, and drill and fasten it to the bevel on the inner stem (Photo 31). A temporary 2-inch sheetrock screw with a ¼-inch washer under the head will work well to hold the plank at the proper twist. The ends of all the planks can be left overhanging the stem and transom an inch or so, to be cut off flush later. Fasten the plank to the inner keel and stem bevel with #10 1¼-inch flathead bronze screws, spaced every 4 inches (Photo 32).

- **Materials**
- **Removing the temporary fastenings**
- **Preparing the plank strips**
- **Planking the hull**
- **Applying the fillets**
- **Cutting off the planking parallel to the sheer**

Photo 31 Fitting and fastening the first plank

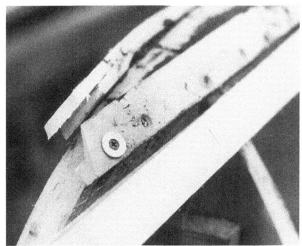

Photo 32 Gluing and edge-nailing the planking

How to Build The Ocean Pointer

Photo 33 Time to begin making epoxy fillets between frames and planking

Photo 34 Planking progresses

Photo 35 Slotted plywood clamp aligns planking between the frames

You now have the first two planks fastened to the boat, with only about ninety to go. At this stage, extra hands will be helpful. You will need a good supply of disposable rubber gloves, and rags and alcohol to clean your tools.

The planks will need to be beveled in places, to make a good fit to the previous plank. You can use a small section of planking stock as a gauge to help you to judge how much bevel is needed at each station. Hold it flat on the frame up against the previous plank, and note how large the gap is—no need to measure it exactly. I like to just eyeball it, marking each measurement roughly on the new plank at each station, then plane the bevel with a block plane. You can check the bevel by holding or clamping the plank up against the previous plank. It doesn't need to be perfect, since each plank will be edge-glued to the next with thickened epoxy, which has good gap-filling qualities.

Once you are happy with the bevel, it is time to mix up a batch of epoxy. Before you add thickeners, paint some unthickened epoxy on the edge of the plank that is already on the boat, and on the bulkhead frame where the new plank will be landing. Then add colloidal silica to the remaining epoxy to a thin peanut-butter consistency. Paint the thickened epoxy onto the edge of the new plank, and then apply it liberally to the bulkhead frame, transom, and stem bevel. Don't forget to put glue in the kerf in the forward end of the plank. Tack the plank in place amidships and back aft, and begin twisting and nailing it edgewise to the previous plank with threaded nails spaced on 8-to-10-inch centers. Work your way forward from amidships, nailing the plank to each frame as you go; then do the same thing from amidships aft. You are nailing the forward half of the plank first because once in a while a plank may break due to the severe twist and bend; the broken plank will be easier to remove if it hasn't already been nailed to the boat back aft.

It is very important that you keep the planks fair in between the frames as you are nailing them on. If you are not careful, you can get flat spots that will be difficult to fair after the planking is complete. Before you nail, sight the plank edgewise to be sure that it is bending fair. You can make some handy clamps to hold the planks in place while you are nailing. These slotted clamps work like old-fashioned straight clothespins, and are made from scraps of ¾-inch plywood (Photo 35). Cut out a dozen or more rectangular pieces about 2½ inches by 4 inches, and cut a lengthwise slot in one end about 2½ inches long. The width of the slot should be about 1/64 inch more than the planking thickness—a full ¾ inch in this case.

These clamps can be slid over the edge of the plank you are nailing, and lapped onto the previous plank to hold the new plank in place. Friction will help to keep the planks from slipping.

Applying the fillets

After you have nailed four or five planks on each side, you should take a short break from planking and mix up a batch of peanut-butter-style epoxy for the fillets (Photo 33). These are applied to the inside corners where the planking meets the frames, to increase the glue area. You will want to stop after every four or five planks to make the fillets; otherwise, if you plank too far you won't be able to reach your hand in far enough to start the new fillet where you left off.

Cutting off the planking parallel to the sheer

As the planking approaches the turn of the bilge, you will notice that the planking line is progressing most rapidly at the stem (Photo 34). If you were to continue planking, the planks would reach the sheerline at the stem long before it reached the sheer amidships, where the girth is greatest. To compensate for the difference in girth, you could taper all the strips towards the bow, but this is very labor intensive. An easy solution is to plank the hull part way using parallel-sided strips, and then to cut off the planking at the turn of the bilge in a curve that is parallel to the sheer. From that point, the planking can commence with parallel-sided strips and come out even at the sheer.

The cutoff line should be located about 17 inches below the sheer. Before the planking progresses too far up the stem, make a mark on each frame and on the stem and transom, 17 inches below the sheerline (Photo 36). Use a thin, flexible batten of wood 17 inches long, bending it around the outside of each frame to mark the 17-inch measurement. Then staple some plastic or wax paper to the frames between the marks and the sheer so that the planks will not be glued to the frames beyond the 17-inch mark. You will be planking beyond the 17-inch marks forward and aft until you have reached those marks amidships. Use sheetrock screws with washers to fasten the planking temporarily to the molds between the cutoff line and the sheer. After you have planked beyond the marks on both sides, let the epoxy cure before you remove the temporary screws from the frames.

Then, use the 17-inch batten again to mark for the cutoff line on the outside of the planking, and connect the marks with a long batten tacked to the planking at each frame. When the long bat-

Photo 36 Planking marked 17 inches from sheer at each frame in preparation for cutting off

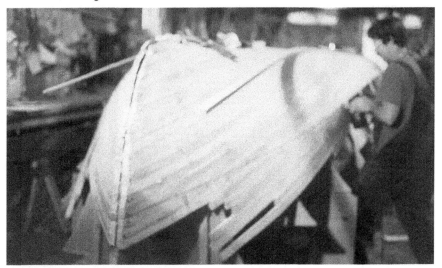

Photo 37 Cutting off the planking parallel to the sheer

Photo 38 One side cut off; batten fastened to other side for marking cutoff line

How to Build
The Ocean Pointer

Photo 39 First plank being fastened after cutting off

Photo 40 All planked (whew!)

ten is fair, and parallel to the sheer, mark the cutoff line on the planking, remove the batten, and cut the planking off with a circular saw, making sure that the depth of the saw cut is set to the planking thickness (Photos 36 through 38). Use an old carbide blade in the circular saw, and wear eye protection, since you will be cutting through many edge nails as you go.

Remove the excess planking below the saw cut, and set all the cut off nails with a nail set. Then clean up the edge using a small rabbet plane so that the edge of the next plank will fit well. Then continue planking as before until you reach the sheer (Photos 39 and 40). You may find that the spacing doesn't work out exactly for the width of the sheerstrake. You can make it up to 2 inches wide if necessary, in order to reach the sheer marks at each station. The sheerstrakes should actually lap past the sheer, especially forward of amidships, to allow for planing the bevel on the top edge to the camber of the deck. Instead of edge-nailing the sheerstrake, screw it edgewise to the previous plank with long sheetrock screws. These can be removed after the glue has cured to allow the bevel to be planed on the top of the sheerstrake.

Chapter VII
Completing the Exterior

Materials

Fairing—

Two 15-ounce tubs WEST System #407 Low-Density Filler

Four 40-grit resin-backed 8-inch sanding discs

Two pieces glass-foam insulation, 4 inches by 18 inches by 4 inches—see Appendix I

Twenty-five sheets 40-grit sandpaper

Ten sheets 80-grit sandpaper

Spray adhesive

One gallon marine oil-based white undercoater

Stem and forefoot fastenings—

Six #14 flathead bronze wood screws, 3 inches long

Four #14 flathead bronze wood screws, 2½ inches long

Four ½-inch bronze carriage bolts, 6 inches long, with nuts and washers

Two quarts bottom paint

Fairing the hull

The first step is to trim off the hood ends of the planking where it overhangs the inner stem and transom (Photo 41). Use a sharp crosscut handsaw, and be cautious so as not to cut into face of the transom with the saw. To be safe, leave a full 1/16 inch and do the final trimming with a block plane. When planing the hood ends at the stem, try to keep the plane square to the centerline of the boat to make it easier to fit the outer stem and forefoot. Once the hood ends are trimmed, you are ready to fair the hull.

An 8-inch circular sander with a soft pad works well for the initial sanding. Use a 40-grit resin-backed disc, and keep the sander moving. Don't tilt the disc on edge; keep it flat on the hull at all times to avoid gouging. You will find that you can keep the sander from wobbling if you put a little extra pressure on the side of the disc that is away from you, while keeping it flat. Don't get too carried away with the power sander—it can remove a lot of material very quickly. It is better to work over the entire hull in several stages, rather than trying to do the final sanding in one operation. Your goal with the power sander is to knock off all the major high spots, and to remove the excess epoxy. When this is done, it is pointless to power-sand any further because the disc is too small to get the hull really fair.

- **Materials**
- **Fairing the hull**
- **Installing the outer stem and forefoot**
- **Flipping the boat**

Photo 41 Hood ends trimmed

How to Build
The Ocean Pointer

Photo 42 Hull faired and undercoated

Photo 43 Outer stem pieces fitted

Before continuing with the fairing, it is time to vacuum the dust from the hull and fill all the nail and screw holes, as well as any major low spots using epoxy resin thickened with WEST System #407 filler. After this has cured, you can remove the bulk of the fairing compound with the power sander before continuing the fairing by hand.

It takes sweat and perseverance to get the hull fair from this stage. The traditional method is to use a "torture board," which is simply a long, flexible board with sandpaper stuck to it. I make mine 4¼ inches wide by 22 inches long to take two half sheets of sandpaper, cut lengthwise. Spray adhesive works well to stick the sandpaper to the board; 40-grit is a good place to start with the torture board. For several years we have been using blocks of glass-foam insulation (see *WoodenBoat* No. 126), instead of torture boards. We call them "fartblox" because of the sulfurous odor that they emit while in use, but we are able to forgive this trait because they work so much better than torture boards. These glass-foam blocks cut as quickly as 50-grit sandpaper, and leave a finish as smooth as 120-grit. Wear a dust mask to protect against breathing in the glass dust that is generated as the foam blocks wear down.

The fairing procedure is the same, whether you are using a torture board or glass-foam blocks. You can begin sanding in a fore-and-aft direction, but work diagonally also—first one way and then the other. After you think you have it looking pretty good, put on a coat of white undercoater. This first coat of paint is sacrificial. It is used just as a fairing tool, and you will sand more than three-quarters of it off before this stage of the fairing is complete. After the paint is dry, begin sanding again. The paint will be sanded off of the high spots almost immediately, but it will remain in the low spots. You won't need to sand all the paint off to get the hull fair, but you should keep working until you see sanding scratches on all the paint that is left on the hull. That is a sign that the sanding board is not bridging any low spots; you are now ready to put on another coat of undercoater.

Continue sanding the second coat as you did the first. You will probably go through to bare wood in places where there are still some high spots, but you should find that most of the hull will remain white, and that the sanding board will be mostly fairing the paint instead of bare wood. When you have finished sanding the second coat, apply coat number three. This time you should find that the sanding board is not going through to bare wood anywhere. When you get to this point, the fairing can be considered complete (Photo 42).

Installing the outer stem and forefoot

The outer stem is sawn from three pieces of mahogany, 3 inches thick. Hold your patterns up to the profile of the inner stem to see how everything matches up. Some adjustments will probably be necessary; it is easier to make the adjustments on the patterns first, and then trace the shape of the patterns onto the mahogany. If the patterns are "shy" at any of the joints, you can add material to them using a hot-melt glue gun.

After you have traced the patterns onto the mahogany and cut and planed the pieces to the lines, you will need to do the final fitting of the pieces before they are glued and fastened to the boat. First, fit piece number one to the scarf at the end of the outer keel. When the fit is good, temporarily screw the piece in place, using a few #14 2½-inch bronze screws. Then fit piece number two to the inner stem and to piece number one. Fasten piece number two with a couple more screws, and fit piece number three (Photo 43).

When you are happy with all the joints, drill and countersink for four ½-inch-by-6-inch carriage bolts that will fasten pieces two and three to the inner stem. You can now remove the three stem pieces, mix up a batch of epoxy, and glue, screw, and bolt them in place.

Use a straightedge as a guide to plane the heel of the outer stem flat, and flush with the bottom of the outer keel. Then try the oak forefoot, and trim as necessary to fit it to the outer keel. Bed the forefoot with adhesive sealant, and fasten it to the outer keel with #14 3-inch bronze wood screws (Photos 44 and 45). The profile of the outer stem and forefoot will need to be trued up next, and then the sides of the stem should be beveled. Mark a centerline down the outside of the stem, and then make two parallel marks offset from the centerline ½ inch on each side to give a width of 1 inch at the forward face of the stem. At the heel of the stem, fair this 1-inch width gradually into the 2-inch width of the forefoot. The forefoot will be beveled on the sides, also, for part of its length. I like to leave the stemhead square for the top 12 inches or so, ending the side bevels in a scallop (Photo 44). The scallop can be shaped with a gouge and a spokeshave, and then the whole outer stem can be sanded and undercoated.

By now you are itching to flip the boat over, but it will be easier if you paint the bottom now while she is upside down. There is no need to establish an accurate waterline at this point, just paint from the keel to where the turn of the bilge begins for now. Put two coats on, let it dry, and then you are ready to turn the boat over.

Photo 44 Sides of stem beveled; note scallops near stemhead

Photo 45 Forefoot bedded and fastened

How to Build
The Ocean Pointer

Photo 46 Hull flipped right-side up

Flipping the boat

First, you will need to remove the cockpit molds. They can each be removed in one piece, except for mold No. 11, which will have to be disassembled because of the way it laps around the motorwell sides. After the molds are removed, remove any other fastenings that might be holding the boat to the floor. The boat should now be supported only on the stemhead and the motorwell sides.

Have ready at hand four 2-by-10-inch planks 8 feet long, and some padding (heavy cardboard and old quilts or blankets work well). Then round up at least five able-bodied helpers. Move the boat to one side of the shop, and lean the planks on the opposite workbench. The lower end of the planks should rest on the floor under the sheer. Put lots of padding on each plank, and tip the boat up onto the planks until it is near the balance point. Have three or more people ready to catch and steady the boat as it goes past the balance point. Then hold her steady while the rest of the crew comes around to help lower the boat down slowly. The planks are there mainly to protect the folks who are catching the boat as it is being flipped. Once the boat is resting right-side up on the planks, the planks can be removed one at a time, and the boat lowered level onto the floor (Photo 46). Time to quit work, break out the refreshments, and have a party!

Chapter VIII
Preparing for Decking

Materials

Deck beam mold—one 1-by-8-inch pine or spruce board, 7 feet long

Sealant—two cartridges Sikaflex or 3M 5200

Rubrail fastenings—30 #12 flathead bronze wood screws, 3 inches long

Deckbeams—one piece oak ⅞ inch by 10 inches, 7 feet long; one piece oak 1½ inches by 7 inches, 7 feet long

Carlins—two pieces oak ⅞ inch by 1½ inches, 12 feet long

Coaming knees—one piece oak 1¾ inches by 10 inches, 3 feet long

Breasthook—one piece oak 1¾ inches by 6 inches by 16 inches

Kingplank—one piece oak or mahogany, ¾ inch by 4 inches, 5 feet long

Cockpit and deck sheathing—15 yards Dynel fabric, 63 inches wide (see Appendix I); 5 gallons WEST System epoxy

Planing the sheer

Before you start making shavings, stuff some crumpled-up newspaper into the spaces between the ceiling and the hull. This will help keep wood chips and tools from disappearing forever into the bilge.

The outside top corners of all the bulkhead frames represent the sheerline at the inside of the planking. The top edge of the sheerstrake will need to be planed flush with the tops of the bulkhead frames. The bulkhead frames were cut out with the tops cambered for the deck crown. This camber should be continued to the outside edge of the sheerstrake. A block plane works well for this. Use a "beam mold" as an aid in establishing the bevel (Photo 47).

On Sheet 7 of the plans is a full-sized half-pattern of the "beam mold." Transfer this pattern onto a 7-foot piece of 1 x 8, cut out the shape, and plane it carefully to the line. The beam mold represents the camber at the top of the deck framing. It will be used as a guide for planing the top edge of the sheerstrake, and the tops of the deckbeams, carlins, knees, and transom.

When using the beam mold, always keep the centerline of the mold approximately in line with the fore-and-aft centerline of the boat (Photo 47). When planing the sheer, work alternately from one side to the other until the edge of the sheerstrake is flush with the top of the bulkhead frames. Sight the sheerline from different angles as you plane the sheer to make sure that it makes a fair and pleasing curve without any humps or dips. The tops of a few bulkhead frames may have to be planed or shimmed slightly in order to get a pleasing sheerline.

Fitting and fastening the inner rubrails

After the sheer has been planed fair and beveled to the deck crown, the inner rubrails can be beveled, bent into place, and fastened. This is one of the more difficult aspects of the project because of the extreme rolling bevel that must be planed on the inside face of the rubrail.

Begin with two pieces of oak, 1½ inches square by 22 feet long. You will probably need to scarf shorter pieces to get the length required. The forward end of the rails will be taking a tight bend because of the fullness of the deck line forward. The aft ends of the rails can have small knots and some grain runout, but the forward end should be clear and straight-grained for the first 7 or 8 feet.

- Materials
- Planing the sheer
- Fitting and fastening the inner rubrails
- Dynel cockpit sheathing
- The deck framing

Photo 47 Using the deck beam mold to check the height of the deck framing and the bevel at the sheer

After you have scarfed the rails and cleaned up the joints, the bottoms of the rails can be beveled. This is a constant bevel, and is most easily done on the table saw. Set the table saw on a 20-degree bevel, and mill the rails to the cross section shown in Figure 6. Keep in mind which end is forward, and mill the pieces with the bevels opposite—one port and one starboard. You can save a lot of head scratching later if you label on each rail the forward and aft ends, port and starboard, and also label top, bottom, inner, and outer faces.

Now comes the tricky part. If the hull were wall-sided, you could bend the rails on as they are, and they would fit. But the flare forward and tumblehome aft in this design make it necessary to bevel the inside face of the rails if the outer face is to remain plumb.

Figure 6 should help when it comes to marking the bevels. You will need to mark all the station marks onto the rails, beginning with the forward perpendicular. Bend a batten around the sheer, and mark and label the location of each bulkhead frame on the batten. Then transfer the marks from the batten to the rubrails. The diagram gives the width of the rail at each station.

Here's the really tricky part, so read carefully. Halfway between stations 7 and 8, the inside face of the rail will be square, since the topsides are about plumb at that location. From that point forward, you will be beveling the rail to match the increasing flare in the sides of the boat. As a result, the top edge of the rail will get narrower as you move from station No. 7 to station No. 2. Then from station No. 2 to the bow, the top edge gradually gets wider to compensate for the decreasing flare from station No. 2 forward. The diagram gives the width of the top of the rail at each station, measured from the outside edge of the rail. Mark the width at each station from the bow to station No. 7 on the top of the rail, and tack on a batten to connect the marks. If you plane the inside face from the bottom corner to the line you just drew, the resulting bevel should match the changing flare in the topsides from station No. 7 forward.

You may need to make a vertical saw kerf about 3 feet long in the forward end of the rail to get it to bend more easily. From station No. 8 to the transom, the top edge of the rail remains a con-

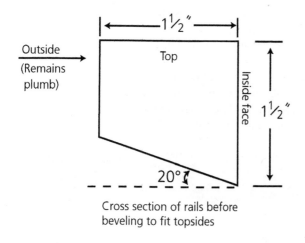

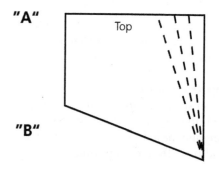

Use the table below to establish the changing bevel on the inside face.

From the bow to Station No. 7 measure width on top of rail from point "A."

From Station No. 8 to transom, measure width on bottom of rail from point "B."

Measure from point "A" on top of rail at each station.

Bow	Sta.1	Sta.2	Sta.3	Sta.4	Sta.5	Sta.6	Sta.7
1 1/8"	7/8"	5/8"	5/8"	7/8"	1 1/16"	1 3/8"	1 7/16"

Measure from point "B" on bottom of rail at each station.

Sta.8	Sta.9	Sta.10	Sta.11	Transom
1 1/4"	1 1/8"	15/16"	11/16"	11/16"

Figure 6 Bevel diagram for inner rubrails

stant 1½ inches wide, but the bottom edge must be planed narrower to compensate for the increasing tumblehome of the topsides. The width of the bottom edge of the rail is given for stations 7 through 11 and the transom, measured from the outside of the rail. Mark these widths on the bottom of the rail, and connect the marks with a batten. Then plane between the line and the top inside corner of the rail to get the bevel to match the tumblehome of the topsides.

Once the bevels are planed on the rails, they can be installed (Photo 48). You will need to bevel the forward end of each rail to fit the sides of the stem. Then bed the rails liberally with adhesive sealant, and fasten them to the hull at each station using #12 3-inch bronze wood screws. Fill the saw kerfs in the forward ends with sealant also, before fastening the rails. You may find that the bevels are not perfect, even with all that careful measuring and planing. While you are scraping off the excess sealant, use your putty knife to fill in any gaps between the rails and the hull. Then use some solvent on a rag to finish cleaning up. The plywood deck will be lapped over the top of the inner rubrails. This means that you will need to get out the deck beam mold again and plane the tops of the rails to the deck camber. With this accomplished, you will be ready to sheathe the cockpit with Dynel.

Dynel cockpit sheathing

This is easier to do before the deck framing and deck are installed. First, fill any screw holes and dents with thickened epoxy, and then sand the cockpit sole and sheathing using 80-grit paper on a soft-pad sander. Sanding will expose fresh wood fibers for a better bond with the epoxy and Dynel.

Sheathing the cockpit sole and ceiling is best done in two operations. Do the sole first, and let the epoxy kick before doing the ceiling. You can roll the Dynel fabric out onto the sole, and wet it out with epoxy, using a plastic squeegee to spread the epoxy and move the excess to drier areas.

It is very helpful to have someone continually mix small batches of epoxy while you spread it with the squeegee. Be careful not to float the fabric with too much resin. Use just enough epoxy to wet out the cloth, and scrape the excess out with the squeegee. Use the squeegee to get rid of air bubbles, which show up as whitish patches under the Dynel. When you do the ceiling, lap the cloth a couple inches over the sheathing on the sole. You may find it easier to hold the Dynel in place on the ceiling with spring clamps, and then wet out the plywood underneath. The Dynel can then be pushed into the wet epoxy, and the wetting out

Photo 48 Inner rubrails installed, kingplank fitted

Photo 49 Aft deckbeams fitted

completed after the cloth is patted into place. After the epoxy has cured, you may grind off any rough edges using a 4-inch angle grinder with a 50-grit disc. The rest of the surface of the Dynel should be left rough, for best nonskid qualities.

The deck framing

Cut out the three deckbeams according to the patterns given. Beam No. 1 will be fitted after the carlins are installed, so set it aside for now. Beam No. 2 will be fastened to the aft face of bulkhead frame No. 10, with its top flush with the sheer. Glue and screw it to the bulkhead frame. Beam No. 3 will be located 15 inches aft of beam No. 2, and will rest in notches in the top forward corners of the motorwell sides (Photo 49).

How to Build The Ocean Pointer

Photo 50 Deckbeams 2 and 3

Photo 51 Breasthook and kingplank installed

Photo 52 Kingplank sprung into notches in bulkhead frames

Its ends will rest on ¾-inch-by-1½-inch cleats glued to the ceiling between bulkhead frames 10 and 11. It will be best to set beams 2 and 3 about ⅛ inch too high when installing them, and then plane the tops to the deck camber using the beam mold as a guide (Photo 50).

The breasthook notches around the stem, and is glued and screwed to the stem and the inside of the planking (Photo 51). Fit the pattern around the stem first, and shape the sides of the pattern to the inside of the planking. Then trace the pattern onto the stock and cut it out with the bandsaw. You will need to plane the sides and the back of the notch to fit the planking and the aft face of the stem. Glue and screw the breasthook in place, then fair it down to the sheer height using a combination of block plane, large chisel, and wood rasp.

The breasthook and bulkhead frames 1, 2, and 3 will be notched for the kingplank (Photos 51 and 52). Center the notches on the centerline of the foredeck. You can spring the kingplank into place and hold it there with a few C-clamps while you mark both edges on the tops of the bulkhead frames for the location of the notches. Make the notches ¾ inch deep so that the top of the kingplank will be flush with the top of the deck. Glue, clamp, and screw the kingplank into the notches, leaving the clamps on until the glue has

Preparing for Decking

cured. Then check the height of the kingplank with the beam mold, planing where necessary to bring it down to the deck camber.

The carlins are next. They will be sprung into the notches in the tops of the bulkhead frames to form the shape of the side decks. The forward ends of the carlins will drop into notches in bulkhead No. 3 (Photo 52). The aft ends will be mortised into deckbeam No. 2. Glue and screw them into the notches, letting the forward ends run past bulkhead frame No. 3, to be trimmed off later (Photo 53). Once the carlins are installed, deckbeam No. 1 can be fitted between them and glued and screwed to the aft face of bulkhead frame No. 3. As with beams 2 and 3, the carlins and beam No. 1 should be set slightly high to be planed off afterwards.

After you have planed the carlins and deckbeams to the deck camber using the beam mold as a guide, you can cut out and install the coaming knees (Photo 54). The patterns give the shape and approximate bevels. First, fit the knees to the deckbeam and carlins, before you cut the arc for the coaming. Then clamp or screw them into place temporarily, and trace the arc onto the piece from the pattern. Then cut out the arcs and install the knees, using glue and screws (Photo 55). Make sure they are installed high enough that the deck camber can be planed into their top surfaces.

Photo 53   Carlins installed

Photo 54   Coaming knees installed

Photo 55   Forward deck framing complete

How to Build The Ocean Pointer

Photo 56 Support cleats for bottom of motorwell

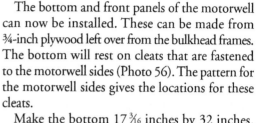

The bottom and front panels of the motorwell can now be installed. These can be made from ¾-inch plywood left over from the bulkhead frames. The bottom will rest on cleats that are fastened to the motorwell sides (Photo 56). The pattern for the motorwell sides gives the locations for these cleats.

Make the bottom 17 3/16 inches by 32 inches. Make the front panel before you fasten the bottom panel. The top edge of the front panel will butt to the bottom of deckbeam No. 3. Cut out the front panel 10 inches by 32 inches, and hold it between the motorwell sides, lapping over the aft edge of the deckbeam. Then trace the crown of the bottom of the deckbeam onto the forward face of the panel and cut it out. Now you can glue and fasten the bottom in place, and then the front panel, which should be flush with the aft edge of the deckbeam (Photo 57).

Photo 57 Bottom installed, front positioned for fitting

It's a good idea to seal all the deck framing once complete (Photos 58 and 59), before the deck is installed. You can use polyurethane floor finish for this. Seal the sides and bottom of the beams, knees and carlins, but don't coat the top surfaces. These should be left bare for better adhesion when the deck is glued down.

If you are going to install a bow eye in the stem, now is the time to do it, before the deck is installed. You won't be able to reach the end of the bolt to put the washer and nut on after the deck is installed.

Photo 58 Aft deck framing complete

Photo 59 Deck framing complete

Chapter IX

Laying the Deck

Materials

Decking—three sheets ⅜-inch marine plywood

Fastenings—two pounds #12 threaded nails 1½ inches long; 100 #8 flathead bronze wood screws, 1 inch long

Marking and cutting out the deck panels

Do the foredeck first. There will be a seam down the center of the kingplank.

Clamp one full sheet to the boat with one edge on the centerline of the kingplank. Mark it and cut it at the bow to notch around the stem. Hold the panel down tight to the sheer, and trace the deck line around the hull onto the underside of the panel. Also trace the curve of the coaming knee and side deck. Cut out the panel, leaving ¼ inch extra all the way around. Use the leftover piece for the stern deck on the opposite quarter.

Now fit the other foredeck piece, and the other stern deck. These four pieces will all lap onto the narrow side decks. Cut them off square halfway between two bulkhead frames. Hold the four pieces down temporarily with sheetrock screws, making sure that they are hanging over the edges ¼ inch all around.

You still need to fill in the side decks, and a piece of afterdeck forward of the motorwell. The side decks can most easily be marked if the foredeck and afterdeck are removed. Before you remove these, make a mark outside the rubrail and inside the carlin to give you the length and angles for the side decks. Then lay the plywood on the side deck framing, holding it down with a few sheetrock screws. Make sure the ends lap past the marks you made where the foredeck and afterdeck end. Trace and cut out the shape, screw the piece back down, and transfer the length marks from the rubrail and carlin to the side deck. Connect the marks with a straightedge and cut the side decks to length. Screw everything back down again for final fitting, trimming the joints where necessary. Then fill in the piece of afterdeck forward of the motorwell. Make plywood butt blocks to back up all the joints. The panels are now ready to be installed.

Installing the deck panels

First, mark the location of each bulkhead frame and deckbeam on the edge of the rubrails; this will help you with the placement of the nails when you go to nail the deck down. Turn all the deck panels upside down, and paint them with a coat of unthickened epoxy. Paint the tops of all the bulkhead frames and deck framing, first with a coat of unthickened epoxy and then with a good, thick coating of epoxy that has been thickened to a peanut-butter consistency.

Screw the panels down with sheetrock screws in the original screw holes, and then nail the panels down to the deck framing and all the way around the sheer into the rubrail. Fasten the butts with bronze screws. Set all the nails, and fill in the holes and any other irregularities with the excess epoxy.

- Materials
- Marking and cutting out the deck panels
- Installing the deck panels
- Sheathing the deck with Dynel

How to Build The Ocean Pointer

Photo 60 Plywood deck laid and sheathed with Dynel and epoxy

Sheathing the deck with Dynel

Plane off the plywood where it overhangs the sheer and cockpit, and round the edges all the way around. Then sand the entire deck with the soft-pad sander, using 50-grit paper. Sand inside the motorwell also.

Sheathe the bottom of the motorwell first, then the sides. If you paint the sides of the motorwell with epoxy, and wait an hour or so until it starts to get tacky, the Dynel will cling to the vertical surface, making the wetting-out easier. Then sheathe the deck, lapping the Dynel a few inches into the motorwell; lap it over the edge of the rubrails and cockpit framing also (Photo 60). Use the squeegee as you did with the cockpit sheathing to move excess epoxy to the dry areas.

Since the Dynel comes only in a 63-inch width, you won't be able to do the whole deck in one piece. To make the best use of the material, the foredeck and aft deck can each be done in one piece, with narrow strips pieced along the side decks. Use a 2- or 3-inch overlap at each joint, and grind the laps flush after the epoxy has kicked. The rough nonskid texture will be lost on the laps after grinding. The texture can be restored by sprinkling nonskid compound onto these areas when you are painting the deck.

CHAPTER X
Completing the Woodwork

Materials

Console, seatbox, and forward seat—

Two sheets ½-inch okoume or fir marine grade plywood

Corner posts—pine or mahogany, 1½ inches by 1½ inches by 20 feet

Forward hatch trim—mahogany, ⅞ inch by 1 inch by 6 feet

Console hatch trim—mahogany, ⅞ inch by ¾ inch by 8 feet

Forward seat drain gutters—oak, ⅞ inch by 1½ inches by 6 feet

Console top—mahogany, ¾ inch by 18 inches by 28 inches

Seat box top—mahogany or other stable hardwood, ¾ inch by 18 inches by 36 inches

Edge trim, forward seat, forward hatch, and console hatch—mahogany, ½ inch by ½ inch by 30 feet

Forward seat framing—oak, ⅞ inch by 1½ inches by 10 feet

Cleat stock—oak, ¾ inch by ¾ inch by 75 feet

Fastenings—200 #8 flathead bronze wood screws, 1 inch long; 1-inch brass brads

Coaming—

Forward section—⅛-inch mahogany veneer, three pieces 10 inches by 10 feet

Aft sections—mahogany, two pieces ⁷⁄₁₆ inch by 8 inches by 9 feet; one piece ⁷⁄₁₆ inch by 8 inches by 6 feet

Butt blocks—two pieces ⁷⁄₁₆ inch by 6 inches by 12 inches; two pieces ⁷⁄₁₆ inches by 2 inches by 12 inches

Fastenings—100 #12 flathead bronze wood screws, 1¼ inches long

Bedding—one cartridge adhesive sealant

Outer rubrails—two pieces oak, ¾ inch by 1³⁄₁₆ inches by 21 feet (may be scarfed)

Bedding—two cartridges adhesive sealant

Fastenings—200 #10 flathead bronze wood screws, 1½ inches long

Motorwell trim—oak, ¾ inch by 1³⁄₁₆ inches by 8 feet

Transom rubrails—two pieces oak, ¾ inch by 1½ inches by 1 foot 6 inches

Spray rails—two pieces oak, ⅞ inch by 2 inch by 6 feet 2 inches

- **Materials**
- **Building the center console and seat box**
- **Building the forward seat**
- **Making the coamings**
- **The outer rubrails**
- **Striking the waterline**
- **The spray rails**

How to Build The Ocean Pointer

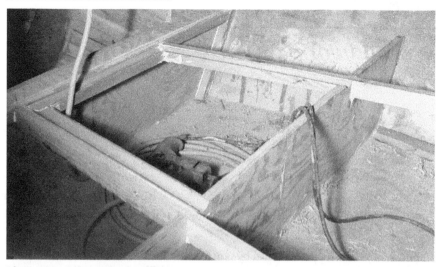

Photo 61 Framing for forward seat

Photo 62 Laminating the forward coaming

Building the center console and seat box

The drawings in Figure 4 (Sheet 3 in the plans) give the dimensions and construction details for the console and seat box. These can both be built as units, and can be installed later. Glue all the joints with epoxy, and be sure to seal the plywood inside. The mahogany top for the console will be permanently fastened. The top for the seat box is removable, with cleats on the underside to keep it in position.

Building the forward seat

The forward seat is a U-shaped affair consisting of two fixed side benches (Photo 72) and a removable center panel (see Sheet 3). The seat is supported by bulkhead frames 4 and 5, and a cleat on bulkhead frame No. 3. Bulkhead frames 4 and 5 have notches in them for the fore-and-aft oak frame pieces. These pieces will sit in the notches, and butt up to bulkhead frame No. 3 (Photo 61). The top corners of these pieces will be notched around the cleat on bulkhead No. 3. Glue and screw the frame pieces in place and cut the aft ends off flush with the aft face of bulkhead frame No. 5.

To keep rain and spray out of the stowage space below the seat, gutters must be installed around the perimeter of the hatch opening (Photo 71). These should be bedded in sealant and screwed to the oak seat framing, flush with the top edge. Use a miter joint for the corners, and cut notches in bulkhead frame No. 4 for the aft ends of the gutters.

Install the fixed side benches on the framing so that the ½-inch plywood pieces overhang the edge and line up with the centerline of the gutter. When you cut out the plywood, don't forget to deduct ½ inch from that edge to allow for the ½-inch-by-½-inch mahogany strips that will be glued on to cover the edge grain of the plywood. Glue and screw the pieces to the seat framing and to the ceiling.

The hatch can then be cut to fit the opening, again allowing for the mahogany edge strips. Install an oak cleat on the underside to keep the hatch from sliding aft.

Making the coamings

The forward part of the coaming will be bent inside the cockpit framing in three or four laminations, depending upon the thickness of the veneer. The combined thickness of the veneers and glue should be 7/16 inch, give or take 1/32 inch. Don't worry about cutting out the profile of the pieces. They can be laminated first, and cut to the shape of the deck after the glue has cured. Have a pile of clamps ready, and some thin wood pads to protect the coaming from clamp marks.

Before you goop the veneers you should make a dry run, bending and clamping them into place to be sure that the laminating will go smoothly. If the dry run goes well, unclamp everything and paint the surfaces to be glued with epoxy. Then clamp it all in place again, making sure that the coaming is plumb, and not leaning inboard or outboard. The angle can be adjusted by edge-setting the pieces up or down. Make sure that the top edge is at least 2 inches above the deck all the way around. When you are happy with the height and angle all around, put a row of spring clamps around the top edge to ensure a tight glue joint (Photo 62).

After the glue has kicked, remove the spring clamps from the top edge, and scribe the cutting line on the top edge of the coaming 2 inches above the height of the deck. A 2-inch-wide block of wood works well for a guide for scribing the line. While the piece is still clamped in place, you can cut to within 1/8 inch of the line with a sabersaw, and then plane to the mark with a block plane.

The lower edge of the coaming will be made parallel to the top edge. This will be easier if the coaming is removed from the boat (Photo 63). Before you remove the coaming, trace the height of the deck on the coaming all the way around the outside so that you will know what height to install it after trimming. Now remove the coaming, set your combination square at 6 inches, and mark the lower edge parallel to the top edge. Saw and plane to the mark, and lay out the fastening location, using the combination square to establish the height for the screws, and a pencil compass to lay out the spacing. Before you fasten the coaming piece in, seal the back below the deck level. Then screw it in, counterboring deep enough for bungs to go over the screws (Photo 64).

Photo 63 Coaming removed for shaping

Photo 64 Aft coaming installed

How to Build
The Ocean Pointer

Photo 65 Coaming butt blocks and running light

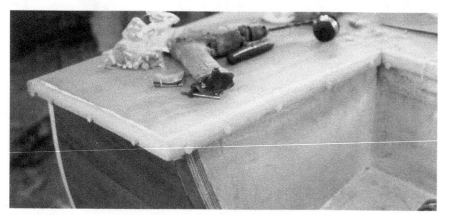

Photo 66 Outer rubrails and motorwell trim

The aft side pieces will be butted to the forward piece, and the joints will be backed up with butt blocks inside and out. Mark and cut plumb the aft ends of the forward piece 8 feet 3 inches from the aft deckbeam. Then cut out the aft side pieces to the shape of the pattern on the pattern sheet, leaving a little wood for trimming. Clamp the pieces into place and fit the aft ends where they lap onto the deck at the aft end of the cockpit. Scribe the top edge 2 inches above the deck and trace the deck height on the outside of the side pieces as you did on the forward piece.

Before unclamping the pieces, draw a line on the deck around the aft ends of the side pieces. You will be putting in a few screws vertically from the underside of the deck into the aft ends of the side pieces where they lap onto the deck. Drawing around the aft ends of the pieces will help you to establish the location for pilot holes to be drilled through the deck so that you will know where to drill for the screws from under the deck. Thinking ahead to the aft coaming that runs athwartships between the side coamings, you can establish the length of this piece by making vertical marks on deckbeam No. 2 where the inside faces of the side coamings meet the forward face of the deckbeam.

Now you can unclamp the side pieces, and mark and cut the bottom edges parallel to the top edge using the 6-inch setting on the combination square. Before you fasten the side pieces in, cut out the aft coaming and clamp it in place, marking the length and angles for the end cuts from the plumb marks on the deck beam. Use a bevel gauge to establish the bevel, keeping in mind that the long point of the bevel will be on the forward face of the piece. When you make the cuts, leave the line to allow for trimming with a block plane for final fitting. This piece will be only ½ inch above the deck instead of 2 inches. Use a ½-inch-thick block of wood to scribe the height. The top corners should be scooped out down to deck level to form scuppers to allow water to drain.

Before you fasten the side pieces in, don't forget to drill the pilot holes through the deck for the vertical screws in the aft ends. Then bed the aft ends with sealant before fastening the pieces. A few shavings off the ends of the aft coaming should give you a good fit there. When you fasten the aft coaming in, it will be best to glue the ends to the side pieces.

Make and fasten the butt blocks next. The outside blocks will be 2 inches wide to match the coaming height. The inside blocks will be 6 inches wide to match the width of the coaming inside (Photo 65). The grain on the butt blocks should run fore-and-aft. If the boat is to have running lights, these can be mounted on the outer butt blocks, with the wires running through grooves in the coamings under the inside butt blocks. Seal the surfaces before bedding and screwing the butt blocks to the coamings using bedding compound and #8 1-inch screws.

If you are careful, the top corners of the coamings can be rounded with the router, using a ¼-inch quarter-round bit. The bottom inside corner can be rounded with a block plane and coarse sandpaper. The screws hole can then be bunged, the bungs faired off, and the entire coaming sanded.

The outer rubrails

The rubrails can be milled to a half-round section with a router or shaper, making two passes with a ½-inch quarter-round bit. Seal the backs of the rails before bedding and fastening.

The motorwell will be trimmed out with the same half-round stock as the rubrails (Photo 66). Use a miter joint at the forward corners of the motorwell. The aft ends of the outer rubrails and motorwell trim will lap past the rubrails on the transom.

Fit the transom rails first. They will need to be scribed and sawn to the shape of the deck crown since they are too short to be bent easily. Bed and fasten them to the transom with the ends overhanging, then cut them off flush with the sides of the motorwell and the topsides of the hull. Next, fit and fasten the trim piece at the front of the motorwell. This piece is long enough to be sprung to the deck camber. Then bed and fasten the outer rubrails and the trim pieces on the sides of the motorwell. Sight the rails from various angles to make sure that they are fair, and adjust up and down as necessary. The aft ends of the rubrails and motorwell trim should then be cut off and rounded to the profile of the transom rubrails.

Note: Because the edges of the deck were rounded before the Dynel was applied, the rubrails should be installed ⅛ inch or 3/16 inch below the sheer. Countersink and bung the screw holes in the rubrails.

Striking the waterline

First, block the boat level athwartships. Then on the transom, measure and mark a level, straight line 6 inches above the bottom. Measure and mark on the face of the stem 40 inches below the sheer. Tack a 6-foot 1 x 3 to the face of the stem with its upper edge on the 40-inch mark, and brace it level. Tack a 7-foot 1 x 3 to the transom with its upper edge on the 6-inch mark.

Pull a string taut across the top of the forward and aft 1 x 3s on both sides of the boat. Then use a level to mark the height of the string on the hull at 2-foot intervals. Remove the string and connect the marks on the hull with a long batten, tacking the batten to the hull and adjusting it up or down to get it fair. Then mark the waterline on the hull with a pencil.

The spray rails

The spray rails will be installed just above the waterline at the stern. Bevel the bottom of the spray rails to a 15-degree angle so that the outboard face of the rail will be narrower than the ⅞-inch inboard face (see Figure 7). Then cut out the rails to the shape of the pattern.

The inboard face will have to be fitted to the hull with a rolling bevel. Trial and error is the best method for planing the bevel. Bed the rails with adhesive sealant, and screw them to the bulkhead frames with #12 3-inch screws. The lower edge of the rail should be on the waterline from the transom to bulkhead frame No. 10, and then be gently curved upwards so that the forward end of the rail is about ½ inch above the waterline. Countersink and bung the screw holes.

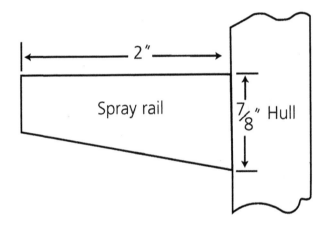

Figure 7 Cross section of spray rail

How to Build
The Ocean Pointer

Chapter XI

Controls, Deck Hardware, and Finishing

Materials

Helm—one Teleflex Safe-T QC helm with 16-foot cable and 90-degree bezel

Splashwell mounting kit—Teleflex part #TEL-SA27253

Steering wheel—one WTR-SW20075*

Controls—one Top Mount control lever

Control cables—two 19-foot Morse 33-C cables, standard or supreme

Motorwell boots—two 3-inch boots

Scuppers—one pair 2-inch-by-6-inch Seastop scuppers*

Running lights—starboard, AQS-3571001; port, AQS-3572001; stern light, AQS-3573001*

Bow chocks—one pair Skene #BKA-01BC600S*

Cleats—one 10-inch mooring cleat; two 7-inch stern cleats

Fire extinguisher

Ventilators—two 3-inch Wilcox vents, model #8799-3 or similar

Battery box

Breaker panel and breakers

Battery switch

*Available from Hamilton Marine; see Appendix I

Painting and Varnishing Supplies

One sleeve each 80-, 100-, 120-, 150-grit sandpaper

One gallon semigloss marine paint for topsides

One gallon semigloss marine paint for deck and cockpit

One gallon antifouling paint if salt water

Two quarts spar varnish

One gallon paint thinner

Japan drier (if cool or damp weather)

Tack cloths

One dozen 1-quart paint pots

Dust masks

Disposable vinyl gloves

Two rolls 1-inch masking tape

One dozen each 2-, 3-, & 4-inch foam brushes

One pint surfacing putty

One quart Interlux #214 bedding compound

Mounting the hardware

Before you start building up paint and varnish on the hull, deck and trim, mount all the hardware for a "dry run." The helm, controls, breaker panel, battery switch, compass, and electronics can all be mounted temporarily on the console before the console is installed. Follow the directions and cutout patterns supplied with each piece of hardware.

- **Materials**
- **Mounting the hardware**
- **The helm**
- **The control lever**

How to Build The Ocean Pointer

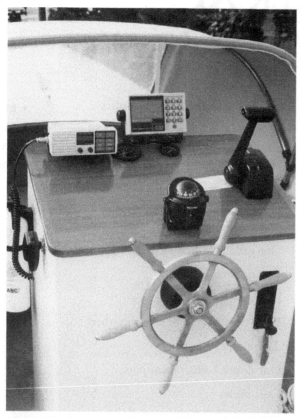

Photo 67 Center console

Photo 68 Testing motor and controls

The helm
Mount the helm in the center of the aft side of the console with the center of the steering shaft 27 inches above the cockpit sole. It comes with a template for the cutout and bolt holes. You can use a hole saw or sabersaw for the cutout. See Photo 69.

The control lever
Mount this on the top of the console on the starboard side, or you can side-mount the control lever on the starboard side of the console. See Photo 67.

The control cables
These will be run through the 2-inch polyethylene conduits that run beneath the cockpit sole. You will need to cut a square hole in the cockpit sole for the control cables to come through into the console. The hole should be about 9 by 9 inches, centered on the inside of the console.

To locate the position of the console, set the console in the cockpit, center it athwartships, and locate the aft face 7 feet 9 inches forward of the inside of the transom, measured along the cockpit sole. Make sure it is square to the centerline of the boat, and trace around the perimeter onto the cockpit sole. Remove the console and cut out the 9-by-9-inch hole in the cockpit sole. You will also need to cut a 4-inch hole in the ceiling on each side in the last bay, between station No. 11 and the transom. Locate the center of the hole about 10 inches above the cockpit sole.

You are now ready to pull the cables. The steering cable will go in one conduit by itself, and the control cables and wiring harness will be run through the other. Start with the steering cable. Wrap some duct tape around the motor end of the cable to help it slide better, and push it into the conduit in the center of the cockpit. Keep pushing until it stops, and then have a helper wiggle and push the cable while you reach into the hole in the side of the ceiling and feel for the end of the cable. If you have large biceps, you may have to enlarge the hole to get your arm in. Grasp the end of the cable and pull while your helper pushes.

The control cables and harness are a little more difficult. They will have to be pulled through the conduit with a piece of electrical cable or an electrician's snake. Lay the control cables and wiring harness out on the cockpit sole, as well as the cables for any electronics that need to run aft. You can also include a piece of heavy nylon twine to use as a snake for pulling more wires in the future. Tape the aft ends of the cables and wires together neatly, push the snake through the conduit, tape it to the aft end of the bundle, and pull the bundle through the conduit.

The splashwell mounting kit

Follow the directions for locating the hole in the side of the motorwell for the mounting kit. Make a hole in the opposite side of the motorwell for the control cables, harness, and fuel line. See Photos 70 and 73.

Scupper drains

You will be cutting holes in the transom for the scuppers. These should be located near the outboard sides of the transom. The bottom of the scuppers will be flush with the cockpit sole. To locate the height, drill a pilot hole from the inside of the transom for each scupper, ½ inch or so above the sole. Then, from the outside, saw down to the level of the cockpit sole using a keyhole saw. Hold the scupper up to the transom and trace inside and outside outlines. Cut out the inside line with a sabersaw, and let the scupper into the transom using a router and rabbeting bit to cut a rabbet to the outside line.

Running lights

These will be mounted on the butt blocks on the coaming (see Photo 65). The wires run through the outer butt block and coaming, and the inside of the inner butt block is dadoed to allow the wires to be run to the underside of the coaming. From there, they can run in back of the ceiling, below the sole, and up into the panel inside the console.

The stern light will be mounted to one side of the motorwell, and the wire run through the conduit with the control cables.

Ventilators

Locate the ventilators in bulkhead No. 3 below the coaming knees.

Bow chocks

Locate these a few inches aft of the stem, and screw them into the inner rubrails. Use plenty of bedding compound (Interlux #214 or equivalent) under chocks and all other hardware.

Panel and battery switch

Mount these inside the console on the port side so that they won't interfere with the control cables. To meet Coast Guard requirements, mount the switch low enough so that the battery cables will be no more than 3 feet long.

Ignition switch

Mount this on the aft face of the console on the starboard side.

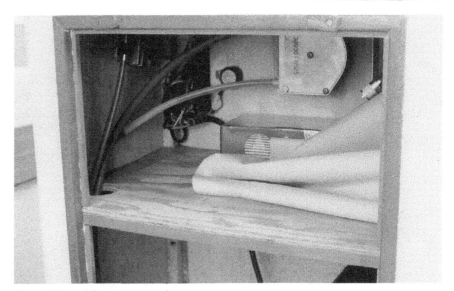

Photo 69 Inside center console

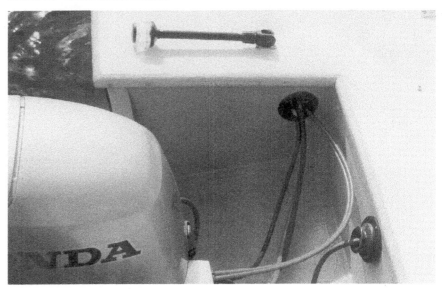

Photo 70 Detail of motorwell showing fuel line, control cables, and wiring harness

Photo 71 Detail of gutters beneath forward seat hatch

How to Build The Ocean Pointer

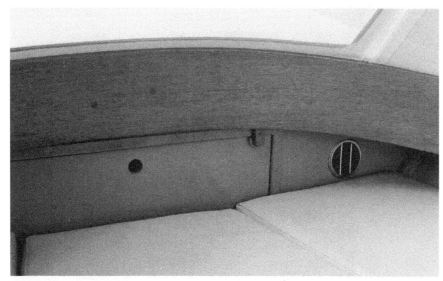

Photo 72 Forward hatch in bulkhead frame No. 3

Photo 73 Detail of motorwell showing splashwell mounting kit for steering cable

Mooring and stern cleats
These can be made of hardwood or purchased. They should be bolted through the deck with carriage bolts or machine screws. Ten inches is a good size. There is nothing worse than a boat with wimpy little cleats.

Fire extinguisher
This is required by the Coast Guard. The port side of the console is a good place to mount it.

Installing the console
Place the console in position, and drill through the cleats on the inside into the cockpit sole for #10 1½-inch screws. Apply thickened epoxy to the bottom of the sole, and screw it down. Make an epoxy fillet all the way around the outside between the side of the console and the sole.

Installing the seat box
Position the seat box a comfortable distance aft of the console with the starboard side flush with the starboard side of the console. Glue and fasten it down as you did the console, with a fillet all the way around.

The battery box
This can be mounted on the sole inside the console on the port side. It must be strapped down securely. If you cut a slot in the sole just inside the wall of the console, a nylon strap can be run through the slot, under the sole, back up through the 9-by-9-inch hole, and over the top of the battery box.

The wiring
To ensure that the wiring is done according to Coast Guard regulations and ABYS guidelines, we recommend that you have the wiring done by a professional. Have the marine electrician rough-in the wiring before you do the painting and varnishing, and then come back to hook up the wires when the finish work is complete.

The fuel tanks
There is room for two portable six-gallon fuel tanks under the stern deck on either side of the motorwell. Run the fuel line through the front of the motorwell just below deck level. It is an easy matter to switch the fuel line from one tank to the other when the first is empty. For extended cruising range, you can either carry extra portable tanks or jerry cans, or if you don't mind losing the stowage space, a fuel tank can be built into the seat box.

Choosing a motor
Mike McConnell used an old 25-horse Johnson to power his Ocean Pointer. We never clocked her from buoy to buoy, but we figure she would do about 15 knots flat out, with a light load. The boat pictured in this book was fitted out with a 50-horsepower Honda four-stroke. We clocked this boat at roughly 26 knots. I say roughly because we were unsure how much current there was in the river during the trials; that figure may be a knot or two off one way or the other. The maximum recommended horsepower is 75. That should push her into the 30-to-35-knot range. Pushing a Pointer hull any faster might prove to be a hair-raising experience. I'm not sure how the boat would handle at higher speeds, and I'd be afraid to find out.

For fuel economy and less pollution, a four-stroke motor is best. The initial cost is higher, but this cost will be more than made up in fuel savings during the life of the motor. Four-strokes are

Controls, Deck Hardware, and Finishing

easier on the eardrums, too—not just yours, but your neighbor's and mine. For best fuel economy, choose a smaller motor and run it at higher rpm's. For a quieter ride and longer motor life, a bigger motor at lower rpm's would be better.

Most motors can be bought with hydraulic tilt and trim. The trim feature is especially handy for adjusting the boat's fore-and-aft trim at different speeds. Ocean Pointer is designed to take a long-shaft (20 inches) motor.

Painting and varnishing

Before you start painting and varnishing, you will have to remove all the hardware. The control cables can stay in place; you will have to work around them when you paint the motorwell.

Before you do any painting, sand all the brightwork down to 120-grit, and apply a few coats of sealer. That way, if you slip with the paintbrush, the paint can be wiped off with a rag without it soaking into the wood.

After the brightwork is sealed, you can start building up finish coats on the topsides. Mask below the waterline with a strip of masking tape, and paint to the tape. Alternate coats of varnish and paint, sanding between coats until you have at least five coats on the hull and brightwork. Save the deck and cockpit for last. Two coats will be sufficient on the deck and cockpit.

Before you paint the deck, seal the joint between the deck and coaming with a bead of adhesive sealant. This should be worked into the seam with a gloved finger and then smoothed with some solvent on a rag. When the paint has dried on the topsides, remove the masking tape and carefully cut in the waterline with bottom paint. The tape leaves a ridge at the edge of the topside paint, which makes the cutting-in easier. If you are careful the bottom paint will follow the ridge, making a clean, crisp waterline.

Finishing touches

Let the paint dry a few days so that it won't be damaged easily, then reinstall all the hardware. This time, bed it all with bedding compound.

Connect and adjust the steering and controls according to the instructions supplied with them. Have the electrician connect the wiring, and test all the electrical components before you launch. While the stemhead is still wet with champagne, test the steering, throttle, and shift controls with the boat tied up to the dock. Then cast off and try her out at low speed first, gradually increasing the throttle when you are sure the controls are adjusted properly. We hope you have packed a good picnic to celebrate a job well done.

Photo 74 Stem detail

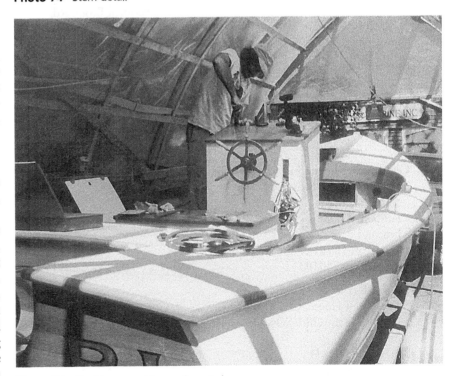

Photo 75 Hooking up wiring and controls

APPENDIX I
Sources for Materials

Marine supplies, hardware, paint, epoxy:

Hamilton Marine
P.O. Box 227
Searsport, ME 04974
800-639-2715
www.hamiltonmarine.com

Jamestown Distributors
P.O. Box 348
Jamestown, RI 02385
800-423-0030
www.jamestowndistributors.com

The WoodenBoat Store
P.O. Box 78
Brooklin, ME 04616
800-273-7447
www.woodenboatstore.com

Davey & Co. London Ltd.
1 Chelmsford Rd. Industrial Estate
Great Dunmow, Essex CM6 1HD
England
Tel: 0117 876361
www.davey.co.uk

Seaware Ltd.
Unit 8b, Kernick Industrial Estate
Penryn, Cornwall TR10 9EP
England
Tel: 01326 377998
Fax: 01326 377948

Combwich Marine Enterprises
Shepards Grove Industrial Estates
Stanton, Bury St. Edmunds
Suffolk IP31 2AR
England
Tel: 01359 251414
Fax: 01359 250103

Wessex Resins & Adhesives Ltd.
Cuperham House, Cuperham Lane
Romsey, Hampshire SO51 7LF
England
Tel: 01794 521111
Fax: 01794 517779
www.wessex-resins.com

Marine plywood:

Boulter Plywood
24 Broadway
Somerville, MA 02145
617-666-1340
www.boulterplywood.com

White cedar strips, ⅛-inch mahogany veneer, oak, ash, and mahogany:

Anchor Hardwoods, Inc.
24B Station Rd.
Wilmington, NC 28405
910-392-9888

John Moody
Little Sheepham, Modbury
Ivybridge, Devon PL21 0TS
England
Tel/Fax: 01548 831075

Newfound Woodworks
67 Danforth Brook Rd.
Bristol, NH 03222-9418
www.newfound.com

Robbins Timber
Brookgate
Ashon Vale Trading Estate
Bristol BS3 2UN
England
Tel: 0117 963 3136
Fax: 0117 963 7927
www.robbins.co.uk

Full-sized patterns for Ocean Pointer:

Stimson Marine, Inc.
RR1 River Road
Boothbay, ME 04537
207-633-6534

Dynel fabric:

Defender Industries
42 Great Neck Rd.
Waterford, CT 06385
800-628-8225
914-632-3001

Appendix II

Repairs and Maintenance

IN THE PREFACE OF THIS BOOK, I wrote about an Ocean Pointer that hit a steel navigational buoy, denting the stem and making a hole in the bottom. After the mishap, the owner was convinced that a fiberglass hull would not have fared so well in a similar collision. Ocean Pointer's stem assembly has a molded dimension of about 6 inches of solid wood, which took the brunt of the impact with only superficial damage. The repair process was simple and straightforward. I'll tell you how I repaired the hole, and the dented stem.

Repairing the hole

The hole was below the waterline, about 6 or 8 feet aft of the stem on the starboard side, and measured about 4 inches wide by 8 inches long. The damage affected a total of five of the 1⅛-inch plank strips. Using a sabersaw with a wide, stiff blade, I cut out a section of each affected plank so that each succeeding plank would be longer forward and aft than the one above it. The top plank of the repaired section was only a foot long, the next one 18 inches, the next 24 inches, and so on—each cutout about 6 inches longer than its predecessor.

Then, instead of making a plain butt joint in each plank, I made a 4-inch-long scarf joint where the ends of the new planks joined the original planks. Beginning with the longest plank (nearest the keel), I made and installed each plank one at a time, using thickened epoxy on all the gluing surfaces, and edge-nailing with bronze ring nails wherever possible. This was difficult on the next-to-last plank because there wasn't much room to swing the hammer, but it was possible with the help of a nail set, and by angling the nails slightly. The last plank obviously couldn't be edge-nailed, but it was only a foot long, and was glued in place around its perimeter. Each scarf joint was held together using a sheetrock screw and a small pad of ½-inch plywood, the pad covering the scarf and the screw going through it and both layers of the scarf. A piece of duct tape on the pad kept it from being glued to the hull. After the epoxy had set, the sheetrock screws and pads were removed, and the new planking planed fair with the original, sanded, and painted. The hole repair took about four-and-a-half hours.

Repairing the damaged stem

The stem hit the buoy about 2 feet above the waterline, and the wood fibers were crushed to a depth of 1½ inches or so. This called for a dutchman or graving piece to be let into the face of the stem where it was damaged.

I cut a 2-inch-deep section out of the face of the stem about 14 inches long, and again, rather than making butt joints, I made a scarf joint top and bottom. The tool of choice for roughing out the cut was a Sawzall, but the job could be done with a handsaw and chisel.

After chiseling the cutout fair, and square, I made a pattern for the dutchman out of a thin piece of wood. This was transferred to a chunk of mahogany, fitted to the stem, and epoxied and screwed into place. After the glue kicked, the piece was faired off with the rest of the stem, sanded, and painted. The repair took about 1½ hours to complete.

Maintenance

When maintaining your Ocean Pointer, the single most important job is keeping the boat clean. Keep dirt from collecting in corners, and cover the boat well when she is hauled out so leaves don't pile up inside.

Every spring, the brightwork should be sanded and varnished with at least two coats, and a third coat in midsummer would be a good idea. Sand and paint the topsides one or two coats every spring, and paint the bottom with antifouling paint if she will be kept in the water. Don't paint the deck and cockpit sole more often than necessary; the paint will fill up the pores of the Dynel, and you will lose the nonskid qualities of the sheathing. If kept clean, they should only need repainting every three or four years.